James K. Polk

James K Polk

Sam W. Haynes

University of Texas at Arlington

James K. Polk

and the Expansionist Impulse

Third Edition

THE LIBRARY OF AMERICAN BIOGRAPHY

Edited by Mark C. Carnes

New York   Boston   San Francisco
London   Toronto   Sydney   Tokyo   Singapore   Madrid
Mexico City   Munich   Paris   Cape Town   Hong Kong   Montreal

Executive Editor: Michael Boezi
Executive Marketing Manager: Sue Westmoreland
Production Coordinator: Virginia Riker
Electronic Page Makeup: Alison Barth Burgoyne
Cover Design Manager: John Callahan
Frontispiece: Culver Pictures
Cover Illustration/Photo: Cover image courtesy of Corbis, Inc.
Visual Researcher: Rona Tuccillo
Manufacturing Buyer: Lucy Hebard
Printer and Binder: R.R. Donnelly & Sons, Harrisonburg
Cover Printer: Phoenix Color Corporation

Library of Congress Cataloging-in-Publication Data

Haynes, Sam W. (Sam Walter), 1956–
    James K. Polk and the expansionist impulse / Sam W. Haynes. —
3rd ed.
        p. cm. — (The library of American biography)
    Includes bibliographical references and index.
    ISBN 0-321-37074-0 (alk. paper)
    1. Polk, James K. (James Knox), 1795–1849. 2. Presidents—United
States—Biography. 3. United States—Politics and government—
1845–1849. 4. United States—Territorial expansion. I. Title. II. Series:
Library of American biography (New York, N.Y.)

E417.H39 2006
973.6'1092—dc22   2005030059

Please visit our Web site at www.ablongman.com

ISBN 0-321-37074-0

1 2 3 4 5 6 7 8 9 10—DOH—08 07 06 05

For Adrian

Contents

Editor's Preface

In 1844, when Democrats met in Baltimore to choose a presidential candidate, the key issue was whether to annex the Republic of Texas. Lewis Cass of Michigan championed annexation; former president Martin Van Buren worried that annexation would lead to war with Mexico. When neither candidate received the requisite two-thirds majority, James K. Polk of Tennessee emerged as an alternative. Though an annexationist, Polk was also a southerner. He won the nomination and eventually the presidency.

When he left office four years later Polk had succeeded beyond nearly anyone's expectations. He had wrested Oregon from Great Britain, vanquished Mexico, and acquired Texas and California. All told, he added 1.2 million square miles to the United States, an increase of over 60%.

Under Polk's presidency, the expansive "destiny" of the United States had indeed become manifest. "Few could have predicted that such dynamic leadership would have been possible at the outset of his presidential term," Sam W. Haynes observes. He adds, however, that Polk's "exaggerated sense of national destiny" carried with it a far higher cost than either he or anyone else could have imagined. The question of whether to allow slavery in these vast new lands ignited the conflagration that became the Civil War. When that bill came due in 1861, it was paid in blood.

This volume goes to press at a time when over 2,000 American soldiers have died in Iraq. Thus a reevaluation of the nation's first foreign war is timely. "Long ignored by historians," Haynes writes, "the conflict with Mexico was characterized by a rush to war, in which political opposition buckled under a zealous executive branch. Early victories led the administration to believe that its mission had been accomplished, only to find that chaotic conditions in Mexico required a much longer military conflict than it had anticipated, leading ultimately to the occupation of a country whose culture it only dimly understood."

History never repeats itself, but the echoes of the past, though distant and dim, often resonate with the present. Haynes's finely wrought biography allows the past to speak with force and clarity.

Mark C. Carnes

Ann Whitney Olin Professor of History
Barnard College, Columbia University

Author's Preface to the Third Edition

The era of Manifest Destiny was a period of profound change for the United States and its neighbors. By the mid-nineteenth century, the United States had emerged as a continental power, while its conquest of Mexico had left a legacy of bitterness in that country that can still be seen today. Prior to the conflict, Americans pointed proudly to their republic as a beacon of liberty, a shining example for other nations to follow. But the war against Mexico—and the spirit of aggressive expansionism that led to it—exposed a far less uplifting aspect of the American character, one that seemed in no way consistent with the principles on which the country had been founded. Marking the beginning of a wider international role for the United States, the war exposed a fundamental dilemma for the American republic in its quest to be both a "good" nation and a "great" one. This problem has only grown more acute during the past one hundred and fifty years, as the architects of U.S. foreign policy have sought to reconcile this peculiarly American sense of mission with the national self-interest. The early challenges of the 21st century suggest that American leaders will continue to wrestle with these often incompatible impulses.

James K. Polk embodied a similar moral inconsistency. The consummate Jacksonian, he embraced the democratic trends that were transforming American society during his lifetime, and which recognized, at least in theory, all white male citizens of the republic as equals. His private writings, however, often betrayed an uncharitable view of human nature. A harsh judge of his contemporaries, he was dismayed when those around him placed self-interest above public duty and community obligation.

And yet, as a man of intense personal ambition, he was noticeably oblivious to his own failings in this regard. Polk never doubted for a moment that he was guided by the purest and most noble of motives, viewing himself as a pillar of moral probity in a grasping and acquisitive world. The pages that follow seek to shed some light on this unwavering self-righteousness, in an effort to make sense of both James K. Polk and the nation he led.

James K. Polk, American expansion, and the U.S.–Mexican War are all topics that have continued to attract scholarly attention since this book was first published in 1996. I have drawn from much of this recent literature for the third edition, especially with regard to Polk's early years in Tennessee. This new edition also reflects some of my own changing attitudes on American territorial growth during the first half of the nineteenth century. The most conspicuous new feature of the book, however, is the addition of study and discussion questions for each chapter. These are not only designed to make students aware of the most important events in Polk's life, but to help them think about the ways in which the eleventh president embodied the values of his age.

One of the most pleasant tasks for any author is to thank those individuals and institutions who have offered support, advice, and encouragement along the way. I owe a special thanks to James Kirby Martin of the University of Houston, who suggested that I write a biography on the 11th president of the United States. A Dobie Paisano fellowship from the Texas Institute of Letters gave me the opportunity to spend six months working on the early drafts of this manuscript in the most delightful of settings—the J. Frank Dobie ranch in the Texas hill country near Austin. Audrey Slate of the University of Texas at Austin helped to make my stay at the Dobie ranch a productive one. I would also like to thank Kit Goodwin and the Special Collections staff at the University of Texas at Arlington, and Richard Francaviglia and Darlene McAllister at UTA's Center for Greater Southwestern Studies. Stephen Maizlish and Chris Morris of the history department at UTA set aside their own research projects to critique my work; I am indeed fortunate to have them as colleagues. I would also like to thank John Belohlavek and Paul Bergeron, accomplished scholars of the period, who read the manuscript in its original form. Both made numerous helpful suggestions and saved me from error more often than I would like to admit. In short, at times this project has seemed like a collaborative effort. Any errors, of course, are mine alone.

Finally, I have the pleasure of dedicating this book, once again, to my son Adrian.

SAM W. HAYNES

James K. Polk

Polk's America

54°40'

Pacific Ocean

Columbia River

Vancouver Island

CANADA

OREGON

49°

TERRITORY

Willamette River

San Francisco

Monterey

MEXICAN CESSION

UNITED STATES

Kearny

Fort Leavenworth

Kearny

Santa Fe

Rio Grande

TEXAS

Fort Jesup

Taylor

Chihuahua

Nueces River

TRANS-NUECES

Doniphan

Corpus Christi

Palo Alto

Resaca de la Palma

Monterrey

Matamoros

Buena Vista

Gulf of Mexico

MEXICO

Scott

Cerro Gordo

Mexico City

Veracruz

Puebla

Donald S. Frazier

The New Arcadia

For a century and a half after the founding of the first English settlements on the Atlantic coastline, Anglo-Americans were in little hurry to explore the continent. In contrast to their French and Spanish counterparts, the early English colonists rarely strayed far from the established communities that hugged the eastern seaboard, as if daunted by the seemingly limitless expanse of land that stretched before them. During the 1700s, the line of settlement inched tentatively westward, but imposing mountain ranges, the absence of suitable transportation routes, and the determination of Native Americans to defend their lands against white encroachment presented formidable obstacles to expansion. By the time of the American Revolution, the advance westward had stalled at the eastern slope of the Appalachian Mountains.

After winning their struggle for independence, many venturesome Americans prepared to take advantage of the largely uncharted transmontane region that Great Britain had ceded to them at war's end. Ready at last to test the geographical limits of their national domain, they now embarked on a migration of epic proportions. Not even the most visionary of observers could have predicted the speed with which Americans traversed the continent. In 1790, a little more than a quarter of a million settlers lived west of the mountains; that number exceeded one million two decades later, and by 1820 more than two million Americans inhabited lands beyond the Appalachian range. As the westward migration rolled forward, gaining momentum and swelling in size, it came to be seen as an inexorable process, ultimately prompting many Americans to conclude that their nation had a "manifest destiny" to dominate the continent.

James K. Polk was born in 1795, just as this great migration was getting underway. The future president spent his earliest years in Mecklenburg County, North Carolina, in the foothills of the Appalachians, some 175 miles from the Atlantic Ocean. At the time of his death a little more than half a century later, the push westward was entering its final phase. With American settlers streaming into Oregon and California, almost 2,500 miles lay between the nation's capital and its farthest outposts on the Pacific Ocean. No American played a greater role in this process of expansion than James K. Polk.

The hunger for land that lay at the very heart of the westward movement was an appetite Polk's forebears knew well; since coming to America from Ireland in the late seventeenth century, the family had engaged in a restless search for cheaper and better farmlands. Captain Robert Polk, a soldier who had married the daughter of an Irish nobleman, established the family along the Maryland tidewater, but it was not long before younger members of the clan moved into Pennsylvania's Cumberland Valley. In the early 1750s they moved again, this time to the North Carolina back country, where they settled along Sugar Creek near the town of Charlotte.

Clannish, fiercely independent, and staunchly Presbyterian, the Polks shared many of the characteristics of the Scots-Irish families who gravitated to the colonial frontier. But the family occupied a higher rung on the socioeconomic ladder than the hardscrabble farmers who eked out a marginal living from the soil. Accustomed to positions of leadership by virtue of their social pedigree, the Polks quickly established themselves as members of the back country elite. Allying through marriage with other affluent North Carolina families, the Polks prospered and became important figures in the political affairs of the region.

When the piedmont became a hotbed of revolutionary unrest during the 1770s, Mecklenburgers turned naturally to the Polks for leadership. In May 1775, Thomas Polk, already one of the most prominent men of the back country, called a meeting to draw up a list of resolves formally severing all ties with Great Britain. With this historic document, the residents of Mecklenburg County became the first Americans to declare their independence from the Crown. In the years that followed Thomas continued to play a leading role in the Revolution, ultimately serving with distinction as a colonel in the Continental Army.

Also signing his name to the Mecklenburg Resolves was Polk's younger brother, Ezekiel. While Ezekiel may have been fired with enthusiasm for independence at the outset, his support for the patriot cause waxed and waned during the years that followed, often as a result of the war's direct impact on his personal fortunes. A headstrong nonconformist, Ezekiel in 1775 disobeyed an order to lead his back country volunteers down to the tidewater region to protect wealthy planters, an act of defiance for which he was temporarily stripped of his captain's commission. Later in the war, as Lord Cornwallis's army swept through the South, Ezekiel remained conspicuously neutral, no doubt in an effort to protect his property from marauding British regulars.

The revolutionary conflict opened up enormous economic opportunities for the Polk clan. Like so many settlers who migrated to the Anglo-American frontier in the late eighteenth century, Thomas Polk and his less distinguished, mercurial younger brother benefited at the expense of the Indian tribes who had long populated the region. The Cherokees, having settled in the area that would later become eastern Tennessee, had taken up arms against the colonial cause during the war, prompting North Carolina to disregard many of their territorial claims. The state established a land office in 1783, by which a handful of insiders acquired land warrants to millions of acres west of the Appalachian Mountains. Not one to shrink from turning his political connections to his own and his family's profit, Thomas Polk managed to acquire preemption rights (options to buy) to thousands of acres in the Duck River valley, a fertile basin of rich, alluvial soil located in central Tennessee. Though unoccupied, most of this territory was still claimed by the Indians as hunting grounds. However, few speculators expected the native tribes to hold on to their title for long. Like other far-sighted investors, the Polks were content to wait for the day when they would be able to take advantage of their new holdings.

In 1784 the North Carolina legislature suspended the land act and closed the state land office, although this did not spell the end of the Polk family's speculative activities. Concentrating his efforts on a special military district that had been set aside to provide headrights for veterans of the Revolutionary War, Thomas Polk used his influence in the state legislature to secure the election of his son William and brother Ezekiel as surveyors for the new district. For their services, the Polks received several thousand more acres of the choice transmontane region.

While Ezekiel benefited handsomely from these transactions, the prosperity he enjoyed owed much to his own industry. A skilled businessman, he operated a tavern, surveyed lands, and increased his land holdings along Sugar Creek, in the southwestern part of Mecklenburg County.

As the years passed, Ezekiel's sons grew to manhood, married, and, with their father's help, established themselves as members of the thriving rural community. In 1794, Ezekiel presented his second son, Samuel, with a nearby 250-acre farm upon his marriage to Jane Knox, the daughter of a local Revolutionary War hero. The couple's first child, James Knox Polk, the first of nine children, was born on November 2 the following year.

Inheriting his father's business acumen but not his impetuous nature, Samuel Polk was soon thriving as a planter, surveyor, and land speculator. With regard to spiritual matters, however, the father and son were of like mind, sharing a profound contempt for their neighbors' unquestioning adherence to Presbyterian orthodoxy. In the wake of a series of tragedies in Ezekiel's life—the death of his first wife and the infant deaths of several children from his second marriage—the elder Polk became disenchanted with the rigid precepts of Calvinism, a faith that condemned unbaptized infants to eternal damnation. Ever the iconoclast, he shocked his Presbyterian neighbors by embracing deism, a doctrine more commonplace in the salons of Paris than the North Carolina back country. Samuel Polk also became embroiled in a minor scandal that must have been the subject of considerable gossip along Sugar Creek. A less than enthusiastic church-goer, Samuel Polk had evidently been involved in a long-simmering feud with the local Presbyterian minister, and the occasion of James's baptism provided the pretext for a full-blown confrontation between the two men. Angry words were exchanged, and Samuel Polk stormed out of the church, taking his wife and son with him, before the ceremony could be performed. The incident must have been the source of deep mortification for Polk's intensely devout wife, who would never have the satisfaction of seeing her son formally admitted into the Presbyterian church.

The post-revolutionary years saw the gradual whittling away of Cherokee claims to Middle Tennessee, as Thomas Polk and his business associates had predicted. Although the national government signed several treaties with the Indians and showed a willingness to honor them, it could not control land-hungry settlers who, aided and abetted by local politicians, pushed westward without regard for federal treaties. Soon after North Carolina finally ratified the Constitution in 1789, the new government in Philadelphia organized the Tennessee country as the Southwest Territory. A treaty with Indian leaders was signed in 1791, by which the United States promised to "solemnly guarantee to the Cherokee nation, all their lands not hereby ceded."

When Tennessee entered the Union as the sixteenth state in 1796, however, the treaty line had not yet been formally drawn. A survey undertaken the following year revealed that it was already obsolete, more than 2,000 settlers having crossed the line into Indian territory. The Adams administration took steps to forcibly remove whites living west of the line, a move that met with vigorous protests from the Tennessee legislature. Reluctant to provoke a confrontation with state authorities, the national government dispatched commissioners to negotiate an agreement by which the Cherokees would cede additional parcels of land, but these concessions were still not enough to slow the ongoing process of white encroachment. With the election of Thomas Jefferson in 1800, the federal government's attitude toward Indian territorial sovereignty underwent a profound change. Though he often expressed concern for Indian rights, the new president was a fervent advocate of American expansion, viewing the West's untapped agricultural potential as the young republic's greatest resource. Increasingly, federal authorities sided with state officials to bring pressure to bear on tribal leaders to cede what remained of Indian claims to Middle Tennessee.

In 1803 the restless Ezekiel pulled up stakes again, and with four of his children and their families made the hazardous journey across the Appalachians to settle a tract of land he had acquired as a surveyor for the military district. Samuel declined to join the family exodus, reluctant to turn his back on a promising future in Mecklenburg County, where he had amassed considerable land holdings and served as a justice of the peace. But in 1805 and 1806, Cherokee chiefs, some of whom had been bribed with money and choice tracts of lands, entirely relinquished their claim to the Middle Tennessee region. Now able to take full advantage of the preemption rights to land he had obtained more than two decades earlier, Ezekiel and his ever-growing family moved again. This time he convinced Samuel to join them.

The opening up of Middle Tennessee's remaining Indian territories to white settlement sparked a land rush, prompting Anglo-Americans throughout the southeastern states to head west in search of cheap lands and a fresh start. From North Carolina, Samuel Polk and his family joined the phalanx of settlers wending its way west along the trails of the Blue Ridge Mountains. The town of Knoxville, in east Tennessee, quickly became a bustling commercial center, its streets jammed with the carts and wagons of immigrants stocking up on supplies before setting out on the final leg of their journey.

Ezekiel, Samuel, and the rest of the clan now settled along the Duck River in newly formed Maury County. With the aid of a few slaves, the Polks proceeded to carve a place for themselves on the raw frontier, clearing forests, planting tobacco and cotton, and building crude cabins. The first years were hard ones for the family. Manufactured goods were a luxury; the necessities of life they produced themselves. But even as the Polks struggled to re-create the world they had known in North Carolina, a new wave of settlers was carrying the frontier line well beyond Maury County into western Tennessee. Within a few years the Duck River region took on a pastoral appearance, while Columbia, the county seat, quickly evolved from a cluster of makeshift cabins into a thriving country village.

As Middle Tennessee flourished and became integrated into an expanding southern economy, the Polks prospered; Samuel Polk would have no cause to regret his decision to join his relatives in the West. Trained as a surveyor, he often received land in payment for his services, and he was soon speculating profitably in the rich farmlands of Middle Tennessee. Ezekiel's son would ultimately serve as one of the directors of Columbia's first bank, and at his death would leave an estate of more than fifty slaves and several thousand acres of land.

The greatest worry for Samuel and Jane Polk as they settled into their new life in Maury County was the health of their eldest son, James. The boy had suffered from a variety of ailments as a child, and since relocating to Tennessee the rigors of frontier life had taken their toll on his frail constitution. Although James sometimes accompanied his father on surveying expeditions, hiking for weeks through rugged terrain, chronic illness required him to spend much of his time at home. Increasingly, the son came under the sway of his strong-willed, pious mother, who raised her son on a steady diet of Presbyterian dogma. In addition to making sure that her son did not adopt the irreligious habits of his father and grandfather, Jane Knox Polk taught him to cope with his infirmities with self-discipline and fortitude. As James matured he turned inward, giving no hint of the frustration that his inability to participate in strenuous outdoor activities with other boys his age must have caused him. Serious and self-contained, he learned at an early age to be the master of his emotions.

As the boy reached his teens, his health continued to deteriorate. He began to suffer severe abdominal pains, which Columbia's physicians were at a loss to explain. Their crude remedies, which probably consisted of purgings and hermetics, failed to bring the boy any relief. The anxious parents were beginning to despair of finding a cure for their son's malady when they learned of a Kentucky surgeon, Dr. Ephraim McDowell, who specialized in abdominal disorders.

A University of Edinburgh-trained physician, McDowell had established a medical practice in the village of Danville, Kentucky, where in 1809 he performed the first successful removal of an ovarian tumor. It would be some years, however, before the international medical community would learn of McDowell's achievements, and even longer before it could believe that such pathbreaking work was actually being performed on the fringes of the Anglo-American frontier. Nonetheless, McDowell enjoyed a growing reputation west of the Appalachians, and in 1812 Samuel Polk and his 17-year-old son made the 250-mile trip by horseback to Danville to see if there was anything the renowned doctor could do for the boy.

McDowell had little difficulty making his diagnosis: Polk was suffering from a urinary bladder stone. The youth was in such frail health, however, that McDowell prescribed a period of rest before risking the operation. Invasive procedures of any kind during the nineteenth century were invariably harrowing and perilous ordeals. Because of the intense pain the patient experienced—whisky was the most common anesthetic—surgeons had to work with great speed, using clumsy implements. Even if an operation went smoothly, the risk of fatal complications was high, since surgeons, as yet unaware of the germ theory of disease, routinely exposed their patients to life-threatening infections.

Several weeks passed before the doctor decided that Polk was finally strong enough to undergo the trauma of an operation. The doctor's assistants strapped the patient to a wooden board, then held his legs high in the air to enable McDowell to cut through the prostate gland and into the bladder. While his patient writhed in agony, if he had not already passed out from the excruciating pain, the doctor proceeded to locate the stone, which he then extracted with forceps.

The surgical procedure was a success and marked a turning point in Polk's life. Although he would never enjoy robust health, the youth began to exhibit a new-found energy soon after the operation. His thoughts now turned to plans for the future.

Realizing that his frail son was not cut out to be a planter, Samuel Polk decided that a career in commerce might be a suitable occupation and secured for him a job with a Columbia merchant to learn the trade. Polk showed little interest in the work, and after only a few weeks won his father's consent to pursue a formal education. Although well behind other students his age, the youth enrolled at the nearby Zion Church Academy, where he quickly demonstrated an aptitude for Latin. Having never developed the physical attributes so highly prized in a frontier culture, Polk found in academics the opportunity to distinguish himself; here at last was an environment in which his talents could be recognized and appreciated. Throwing himself into his studies, Polk showed such promise that a year later his father agreed to send him to the Bradley Academy in Murfreesboro. Here, too, he excelled, so much so that after a year at the academy he set his sights on obtaining a college degree.

In January 1816, Polk traveled to the University of North Carolina at Chapel Hill, a school of approximately 80 young men where his father's cousin, William Polk, served on the board of trustees. Although Polk passed the entrance examination with such distinction that he was admitted as a sophomore, at 20 years of age he was still older than most of his classmates. The years Polk had lost to illness had not been wasted, however, for they had given him a mental toughness and a resolute will that others lacked. With a zeal not uncommon among late-starters, Polk sought to make the most of his college education. His self-discipline and tireless diligence enabled him to outshine those who may have possessed greater innate ability. Not content to excel in his coursework, Polk emerged as a student leader, serving as president of one of the school's two debating societies. Having arrived at Chapel Hill an unpolished youth with little formal education, Polk would graduate first in his class two and a half years later, receiving highest honors in mathematics and the classics.

In the fall of 1818 Polk returned to Tennessee, brimming with a new self-confidence and intent on pursuing a career in law, which he no doubt hoped would lead to political opportunities. He was fortunate to obtain a position in the Nashville law office of Felix Grundy, the most famous criminal lawyer in Tennessee. A self-educated, backwoods attorney, Grundy relied more on folksy humor than legal technicalities to win over rural juries and was reputed never to have lost a capital murder case.

Polk had just begun his law studies when the country found itself in the grip of a severe depression. The national economy had grown at a dizzying rate since the end of the War of 1812, due largely to a surge in demand by British textile mills for short-staple cotton. In recent years, thousands of Americans had headed into the transmontane region, where rich, cotton-growing lands could be had at low prices, to take advantage of the boom. The Bank of the United States and a horde of newly chartered, unregulated state banks had fueled the region's explosive growth with liberal credit, sparking a speculative mania that sent land prices soaring upward. But in 1819 the price of cotton fell sharply, carrying land values down with it, which led to the complete collapse of the credit-built economy.

The nation's economic pulse would slowly return to normal after the Panic of 1819, but American politics would never be the same. Roused to action, desperate voters blamed their elected representatives for the crisis and proceeded to turn them out of office in astonishing numbers. It soon became clear that the public outcry for reform was not a temporary phenomenon, but rather the first phase of a political revolution that would ultimately transform state and national government. No longer willing to put their trust and confidence in men whom they once regarded as their social "betters," voters now sought to elect men of their own station and socioeconomic backgrounds. In Tennessee, as in other western states hard-hit by the panic, voters rallied behind a new breed of political leaders who promised to address the concerns of the small farmer while railing against the monied elites whom they accused of causing the depression. Felix Grundy, who had formerly served as a congressman in his native state of Kentucky, was among the first public figures to sense the changing political mood and turn it to his advantage. Campaigning for debtor relief, Grundy rode a wave of popular discontent to a seat in the state senate. A new era of increased participatory democracy had arrived.

For the ambitious young law student, the chance to pursue his interest in politics presented itself much sooner than he could have imagined. On learning that the position of senate clerk was available, Polk immediately pressed

Grundy into using his considerable influence in the legislature to help him win the job. Polk's chief function was to keep a careful record of the senate's deliberations. Thorough and methodical, Grundy's young protegé was ideally suited for the work. The position offered Polk an invaluable apprenticeship, enabling him to study the inner workings of the political process at close hand and giving him the chance to work with some of the state's leading lawmakers.

Since the legislature met in its regular biannual session or in special session at most for only a few weeks each year, Polk had plenty of time to concentrate on his law studies, and in 1820 he was admitted to the bar. Establishing a practice in his home town of Columbia, Polk soon had as much business as he could handle. Although bruised by the economic downturn of 1819, the Polk family's fortunes had rebounded quickly, and Samuel Polk's real estate ventures required legal services for which he turned, naturally enough, to his eldest son. When the last of the Chickasaw lands were opened up for sale in west Tennessee in 1819, the Polks were once again quick to obtain some of the territory's choicest acreage.

While Polk would continue to practice law throughout much of his career, the occupation held little attraction for him, serving principally as a means to subsidize his real vocation—politics. By 1822, the 27-year-old attorney was ready to throw his own hat into the political arena and announced his candidacy for a seat in the lower house of the legislature. The prominence of the Polk family proved to be an invaluable asset for the young political aspirant. Even so, Polk left nothing to chance and spent the next several months canvassing Maury County, riding from farm to farm in an effort to win over voters. The district's incumbent representative was unable to mount an effective campaign against so well connected and determined a challenger, and Polk was elected by a comfortable margin.

The steady income Polk derived from his law practice not only allowed him to indulge his passion for politics, but to entertain thoughts of matrimony. While attending legislative sessions in Murfreesboro, Polk found time to court Sarah Childress, the dark-haired sister of one of his former classmates at the Bradley Academy. Her father had been a prominent local merchant and planter, who before his death sent his daughters off to finishing school to cultivate what were then known as "the feminine arts," such as needlework, music, and poetry. Like Polk's mother, Sarah was a woman of unbending Presbyterian convictions, viewing all forms of amusement and recreation on Sundays as violations of the sabbath. Nonetheless, she possessed a simple charm and gregarious manner that contrasted sharply with her stiff, intensely serious suitor, allowing her to shine on social occasions. A young woman of keen intelligence and quick wit, she had the ability to speak her mind without seeming outspoken, to assert herself without defying the boundaries of convention that so narrowly defined roles for women in the early decades of the nineteenth century.

The fall of 1823 was a busy one for Polk, who took his seat in the legislature and made plans to marry Sarah (they were wed on New Year's Day, 1824). The young representative from Maury County promptly allied himself with the forces of reform in the legislature, which were ably led by the state's governor, William Carroll, and included David Crockett, the colorful state senator from Tennessee's newly formed Western District. Polk found himself at odds on most issues with his mentor Felix Grundy, whose enthusiasm for debtor relief and democratic reform had cooled since his election, although the pair remained close friends. The freshman representative was particularly active in a movement to rewrite the state's constitution, joining with a group of reformers in calling for a constitutional convention to democratize county government and make the tax system more progressive. Despite the broad-based support for political and economic change, however, the reform faction was unable to muster the two-thirds majority of the legislature needed to hold a constitutional convention. A decade would pass before a new state constitution would be enacted to reflect the sweeping changes of the new democratic revolution.

Even at this early stage in his career, Polk was developing a political credo to which he would adhere faithfully with few modifications in the years ahead. The young legislator subscribed to a Jeffersonian agrarian philosophy, one which viewed the young republic as a new arcadia, free of the vice and corruption of Europe. The pastoral world he sought to preserve required no special legislative action in order to flourish, its self-reliant citizens asking little of their government but a simple guarantee of liberty. It was the natural tendency of strong governments, on the other hand, to abuse their power, promoting the interests of a privileged few. Only by resisting the temptation to increase its authority, Polk believed, could a responsible government guard against such evils.

To be sure, Polk's family had reaped large rewards from the clan's extensive network of political connections, the very advantages that good, virtuous republicans abhorred. But while the Polks of Maury County were more affluent than many of their neighbors, they could not be considered frontier oligarchs. Unlike his older brother Thomas, Ezekiel had not enjoyed direct access to the circles of power in North Carolina. James K. Polk's forebears owed their success as much to thrift and hard work as to the special favors they had received from politically prominent relatives. Different as he was from his grandfather Ezekiel, the doughty pioneer, and his father Samuel, the savvy entrepreneur, Polk shared with them an uncompromising work ethic, which held that worldly goods were a measure of individual worth only if they had been attained by honest labor.

While Polk's solid performance in the 1823 legislative session marked him as a rising star in local politics, the sudden and meteoric appearance of another Tennessee candidate for public office was attracting national attention. A prominent group of speculators had hit on the idea of fielding General Andrew Jackson, the popular hero of the War of 1812, in the 1824 presidential election. Initially, Jackson's campaign for the nation's highest office was given scant chance of success; indeed, even some of his closest supporters privately seem to have backed his candidacy in an attempt to gain political advantage in their home state. Once set in motion, however, the move to draft Jackson took on a life of its own; the democratic stirrings that had been felt in the wake of the Panic of 1819 now erupted in a groundswell of support for the country's most renowned military figure.

Andrew Jackson was in many respects an unlikely champion of the people. Throughout much of his adult life, he had been closely associated with the state's political and economic power brokers. Beginning his legal career as a public prosecutor, Jackson had served writs of foreclosure with a zeal that displayed little sympathy for the debtor class. Marrying into one of Nashville's founding families, he had amassed an enormous fortune as a planter and speculator. At the time of his nomination for the presidency Jackson had not held political office in two decades, nor had he shown much enthusiasm for the democratic reform movement that threatened to break the power of the state's oligarchy.

But if Andrew Jackson did not truly represent the so-called "common man," there was every reason to believe that he thought he did. Combative by nature and predisposed to see the world as a contest between opposing moral forces, Jackson warmed to his role as guardian of the people's interests. In the eyes of many Americans, Jackson was well suited to the task; his celebrated victories against the British and the Indians had already elevated him to the status of heroic icon and endeared him to a grateful nation. Equally important, his upbringing on the Appalachian frontier set him apart from the refined, seaboard gentry who had occupied the presidential chair since the founding of the Republic. In an age of expanding suffrage and increased voter participation, Jackson's appeal drew much of its potency from a longing in the electorate for a candidate that it could call its own. Thus was born, curiously enough, a personality cult in an egalitarian age that was to transform American politics.

Reform-minded Tennessee politicians were hesitant to support Old Hickory's candidacy. Polk and others slowly began to clamber aboard the Jackson bandwagon, however, once it became clear that the general was too obstreperous and forceful a personality to be the pliant tool of the conservative faction that had initially backed him. As a preliminary test of Jackson's support in his home state, the general's supporters offered him as a candidate for the U.S. Senate in 1823. By a vote of 35 to 25, with Polk voting in the majority, the General Assembly elected Jackson, thereby enabling the Tennessee hero to clear an important first hurdle in his bid for the presidency. For the next 25 years, Polk would never falter in his devotion to Jackson or the political views with which he would become associated.

As Old Hickory's political machine began to gather momentum, it sought to field a slate of Jacksonians for local and national offices. In Tennessee, the sixth congressional district race promised to be particularly contentious. Amid rumors that Andrew Erwin, one of Jackson's most vocal critics, planned to run for the seat, the general's friends began casting about for a promising candidate to oppose him. James K. Polk seemed a logical choice; he had distinguished himself in his first legislative session and could rely on a solid base of support in Maury, the second largest of the four counties that comprised the district. The situation was complicated, however, by the fact that there was no shortage of pro-Jackson contenders for the seat. Polk announced his candidacy in the summer of 1824, but in the months ahead no less than four other Jackson men declared their intention to run against Erwin.

The roster of candidates in the sixth congressional district would not be finalized until after the presidential contest had been decided. In 1824, Andrew Jackson faced three strong challengers: Henry Clay, the Speaker of the House; William Crawford, Treasury secretary; and John Quincy Adams, the secretary of state. A fourth, John C. Calhoun, enjoyed little support outside his home state of South Carolina and decided to settle for the vice-presidency. The Tennessean managed to win a plurality of the popular vote, but lacked a majority in the electoral college. It thus fell to the House of Representatives to decide the outcome. Ignoring Jackson's mandate, the House handed the election to John Quincy Adams, who had polled second in the crowded field. At first the Jackson camp accepted the verdict, but when Adams subsequently tapped Henry Clay to serve as his secretary of state, Jackson's supporters cried that the two men had conspired to rob their candidate of the presidency.

The election controversy undoubtedly helped pro-Jackson candidates in the 1825 congressional races, and Tennessee's sixth district race in particular. Andrew Erwin was related by marriage to Henry Clay, now vilified for his role in what many referred to as a "corrupt bargain." Nonetheless, Polk faced an uphill battle in his first bid for national office. He was little known outside Maury

County, and although one candidate had been persuaded to withdraw, Polk still had to compete with three other contenders for the pro-Jackson vote.

Little about the young state legislator suggested the bright political future that lay ahead of him. Polk lacked the affable temperament and outgoing manner that were indispensable qualities for those seeking public office in this new age of democratic politics. A man of stiff dignity and icy reserve, the college-educated Polk had little in common with his district's rural, often boisterous voters. Below medium height and slender in build, Polk did not cut a particularly imposing figure; his erect bearing and thin, tightly drawn lips were the only signs that betrayed the unbridled ambition that raged within him. Nor was he a particularly gifted public speaker. His earnest, declamatory style had won high marks in college, but Polk's speeches lacked the rhetorical flourish common among the great orators of his day. "He has no wit . . . no gracefulness of delivery, no elegance of language," John Quincy Adams noted disapprovingly some years later. In short, Polk was an uncharismatic political figure. Unlike such popular idols as Andrew Jackson or Henry Clay, he would never excite the public's imagination or inspire its devotion.

Despite these drawbacks, Polk proved to be a formidable candidate. His strategy in the sixth district race was simple enough: he would work harder than any of his opponents. The unflagging energy and stubborn resolve that had accounted in no small measure for his success as a student at the University of North Carolina he now brought to bear on the challenges he faced on the campaign trail. Determined to master the art of grassroots electioneering, he managed to conquer his shortcomings or in some way compensate for them. Polk made up for his lack of eloquence with unpretentious, straightforward oratory that spoke directly to his unlettered audiences.

On the stump he made every effort to conceal his humor-less manner, larding his speeches generously with amusing anecdotes. These he delivered in somewhat stilted fashion, but effectively enough to charm a crowd. On election day, needing only a plurality to win, Polk led the field with 35 percent of the vote. Polk had not only bested his four rivals; he had triumphed over his own innate defects as a politician. In the end, he had manufactured a believable public persona for himself, a creation of his own in-domitable will.

Servant of the People

In the early decades of the nineteenth century, the citizens of Washington, D.C., proudly referred to the capital as "the city of magnificent distances," a title that suggested sweeping boulevards envisioned by the city's planners. But the capital presented a considerably less impressive appearance than the name implied. Charles Dickens dubbed Washington "the city of magnificent intentions" and ridiculed its "spacious avenues, that begin in nothing, and lead nowhere . . . ." Certain stretches of Pennsylvania Avenue, according to one resident, looked more like "a cornfield than the great thoroughfare and principal avenue of a metropolis." Most visitors commented favorably on the white marble Capitol with its gleaming, copper-plated dome, still in the final stages of completion more than a decade after being burned by the British in 1814. And yet it appeared so incongruous to one observer, being perched on a hill above the village of red brick houses and makeshift public buildings, that it seemed "placed there by mistake."

Cosmopolitan visitors may have scoffed at Washington's grandiose pretensions, but the nation's capital could not have failed to impress the freshman congressman from Columbia, Tennessee, in the late fall of 1825. Polk had journeyed to Washington with some of the other members of the Tennessee delegation, and on their arrival they found lodgings at a boardinghouse near the Capitol. There being no office space available for congressmen in any of the federal buildings, Polk would conduct much of his official business from his boardinghouse room. Like other congressmen of modest means, Polk would find that the cost of lodging and travel consumed much of his salary. To make ends meet, he continued his Tennessee law practice when Congress was not in session.

When Polk took his seat in the Nineteenth Congress, the battle lines between the Adams and Jackson forces were clearly drawn. Polk was a member of the "factious opposition," a solid bloc of Jackson supporters determined to thwart the Adams administration at every turn. Though not yet a member of Jackson's inner circle, the ambitious young congressman maintained an active correspondence with the Tennessee general, keeping him abreast of political affairs in the nation's capital. In his first speech, Polk joined other Jacksonians in proposing to abolish the electoral college, which he believed had enabled Adams and Clay to deny their candidate the presidency. For his part, President Adams did little to soothe the tense atmosphere created by the controversial circumstances of his election by unveiling an agenda that amounted to a wholesale repudiation of Jeffersonian republican principles. A staunch nationalist and advocate of a strong federal government, Adams outlined an ambitious public spending program, which included the building of a national university, an astronomical observatory, and a wide array of internal improvements, all to be paid for with a protective tariff.

Predictably, the freshman congressman from Tennessee took a dim view of Adams's nationalist agenda. Committed to the strict constructionist principles of a limited government, Polk had nothing but scorn for the administration's plans to subsidize educational and scientific endeavors.

He was no less opposed to the idea that Washington should promote economic development, believing that the consolidation of power in the hands of the federal government would lead inevitably to the tyranny of a privileged few. Polk wavered on the question of internal improvements, an issue of great concern to his constituents, who generally favored the building of roads and turnpikes to link the state with new markets. On most issues, however, the congressman remained true to his philosophy of simple and economical government.

The election of 1824 had stalled the Jackson juggernaut only temporarily. In the four years that followed, the general's partisans labored tirelessly to mobilize support for their candidate, and in the process built the most sophisticated political organization the country had yet seen. Campaign committees in every state worked to drum up enthusiasm for the general at the grass roots level. Across the country, stump speakers and newspaper editors portrayed Andrew Jackson as "the candidate of the People" and lambasted Adams and Clay as the agents of corruption and aristocratic privilege. In the presidential contest of 1828 Jackson swept the South and the West, winning by a popular vote margin of 150,000, and by a 2-to-1 margin in the electoral college.

On inauguration day, huge crowds jammed Washington streets for a glimpse of the "Old Hero." After the swearing-in ceremony, the throng trooped down Pennsylvania Avenue for a riotous inaugural reception at the White House. To his supporters, Jackson represented the very apotheosis of the democratic spirit, his election signifying the dawn of a new age in American politics. The young representative from Columbia, Tennessee, had particular reason to feel optimistic about the future. Without children of his own, Jackson assumed a solicitous, paternal interest in the careers of his young lieutenants and had taken a liking to Polk and Tennessee's flamboyant new governor, Sam Houston. Both men would profit enormously from Jackson's sponsorship in the years to come. Undeniably, Polk had hitched his star to the right man.

The harmony within the ranks of the Jackson camp did not last. Even before the inaugural, John C. Calhoun, who had rejected Adams's nationalism and been retained by the new administration as vice-president, and Secretary of State Martin Van Buren began jockeying for position as Jackson's heir apparent. Known in his home state of New York as the "Little Magician," Van Buren cleverly ingratiated himself with the president, while Calhoun quickly fell into disfavor. Matters soon came to a head over the tariff. Van Buren, mindful of the growing support for protectionism among manufacturing interests in the North, sought to prevent agitation on the issue. Opposition to a high tariff in many parts of the South, on the other hand, led John C. Calhoun to espouse the doctrine of nullification, which held that a state could refuse to obey the tariff, or any federal law it deemed unconstitutional. The tariff issue was not Calhoun's only concern. Alarmed by rising opposition to slavery in the North, the South Carolinian sought to protect the institution by steadfastly defending the rights of the southern states against encroaching federal power. Denounced outside the Deep South for its extremism, Calhoun's doctrine was in fact an attempt to pre-empt the more militant, even secessionist attitudes that were gaining ground in his home state.

In the feud between Van Buren and Calhoun, the cautious Tennessee congressman endeavored to steer a middle course. While his states' rights convictions pulled him naturally in the direction of the South Carolinian, Polk was reluctant to side openly with the nullifiers. At a state dinner celebrating Jefferson's birthday on April 13, 1830, Jackson gruffly proclaimed his unequivocal stand against the nullification doctrine with the toast: "Our Federal Union, it must be preserved." Thereafter Polk distanced himself from Calhoun and his supporters, leaving no doubt that he was, first and foremost, a Jackson man.

By this time Sarah had joined her husband in the nation's capital. She had grown lonely in Columbia, their efforts to raise a family having been unsuccessful. The abdominal surgery her husband had undergone many years earlier on Dr. Ephraim McDowell's operating table may have left Polk sterile. Whatever the reason for their inability to have children, it was a great disappointment to Sarah, and to fill this void she began to take a more active part in her husband's career. Well versed in political matters, she would serve as Polk's trusted confidante throughout his career, providing both support and counsel. Moving easily in the capital's social circles, Sarah proved an enormous asset to her somewhat stiff, dour husband, winning admirers among Polk's political friends and enemies alike.

Though childless, James and Sarah maintained strong ties with a large family network back home, and the Polk household in Washington was always open to younger relatives visiting from Tennessee. Since the death of his father in 1827, James had taken on the role of family patriarch, assuming responsibility for the welfare of his youngest siblings. Four years later, when the family was stunned by the deaths in quick succession of three of Polk's brothers, James helped to provide for their children and served as caretaker for their estates. While Sarah lavished attention on the youngest members of the clan, her husband exercised his familial duties with a characteristically stern hand. On learning that William, the second youngest of his brothers, had run up $700 in debts to Columbia storekeepers, Polk promptly packed him off to school in North Carolina, instructing his relatives in the state to keep a watchful eye on the boy. Without guidance and restraint,

Polk feared, "there is every prospect that he will be a spendthrift and possibly become abandoned to other vices." Polk's fears were well founded, and in the years ahead William's prodigal ways would continue to vex his more serious older brother.

The premature deaths of three brothers may have prompted Polk to give some thought to his own mortality and alerted him to the need to provide for Sarah after he was gone. In any event, he now began to take an interest in the land holdings he had accumulated some years ago in Tennessee's Western District, hoping to supplement his congressional income. Polk hired an overseer, placing him in charge of a dozen slaves to clear a 1,000-acre tract of land in Fayette County. Polk relied on his brothers-in-law James Walker and Dr. Silas Caldwell to tend to his business affairs while he was away in Washington. After a poor crop in 1834, Polk sold the plantation for $6000. Determined "to make more money or lose more," he quickly purchased another plantation with Caldwell in northern Mississippi, the doctor later selling his interest to Polk and his brother William. This venture proved somewhat more successful, but as Polk's political fortunes rose he had less time to devote to his business affairs, and he toyed occasionally with the idea of selling all or a part of his Mississippi holdings. Unable to find a suitable buyer, the Polks held on to the land, which continued to provide extra income for the couple in the years ahead.

Finding a reliable overseer who did not require constant supervision to manage his cotton lands profitably proved to be an ongoing problem for Polk. Ephraim Beanland, who managed Polk's cotton holdings in the early 1830s, was one of a number of overseers who failed to meet the Tennessee congressman's expectations entirely. Intent on establishing his authority over the field hands, Beanland administered the lash without restraint, prompting several slaves to run away. "I will be damde if I can do anythinge with them," Beanland wrote in frustration to his employer. Obliged to spend considerable time and effort locating and recovering these runaways, Polk's brothers-in-law were not always unsympathetic to their plight. After a visit to the plantation Caldwell wrote, "Your negroes here are very much dissatisfied," a problem he attributed to Beanland's harsh treatment and intemperate manner. A. O. Harris, who had married another of Polk's sisters, also wrote disapprovingly of Beanland's conduct after the overseer had administered a brutal whipping to Jack, one of the field hands: "I am very much afraid that he will not treat your negroes as you would wish."

Not surprisingly, given his strong religious views, Polk frequently employed the language of the paternalistic slaveholder, yet he allowed his Christian values to intrude upon his business affairs only up to a point. He seems to have taken no interest in the religious instruction of his slaves, nor was he averse to the use of corporal punishment as a deterrent to unwanted behavior. And though he tried to avoid slave sales that would break up families, and set aside a few acres to allow his field hands the opportunity to grow cotton in their spare time, such actions may have stemmed in large part from a desire to be spared the cost and inconvenience of dealing with runaways. Like so many slave owners, in the final analysis Polk was governed less by Christian charity than by economic self-interest, believing that a contented work force was a productive one.

In the closing months of Jackson's first term, the administration became embroiled in a struggle that would place an even greater strain on the Democratic coalition than the nullification crisis. This time, Jackson's aggressive use of executive authority was directed against the Bank of the United States (B.U.S.). Although criticized by many

Americans for its tight-fisted credit policies during the Panic of 1819, the B.U.S. in recent years had enjoyed a reputation for sound management under the direction of its aristocratic young president, Nicholas Biddle. In the absence of a uniform federal currency, the B.U.S., like all other banks at this time, issued notes that circulated as legal tender. Eager to increase their profits, many state-chartered banks resorted to the dubious expedient of issuing notes far in excess of the specie they held on reserve. As the nation's largest lending institution, the B.U.S. had the power to compel these smaller banks to limit the amount of notes they issued, thus promoting economic stability and serving as a much-needed safeguard against inflation.

For Andrew Jackson, the evils of a national bank far outweighed its advantages. The president harbored a long-standing distrust of paper money, having once lost a sizable fortune when he accepted the notes of a business associate that later proved worthless. Convinced that the circulation of paper money enabled a handful of speculators to profit at the expense of honest, hard-working Americans, Jackson favored a hard money policy, with gold and silver coin as the nation's principal medium of exchange. Jackson's anti-bank views stemmed from a sense of anxiety, shared by Polk and many Americans, about a rapidly expanding, impersonal marketplace. By drastically restricting the flow of credit that fueled this growth, Jackson sought to arrest the forces of economic modernization, which in his mind bred inequality and threatened to destroy the arcadian values that nourished the young republic.

As in so many of Jackson's political struggles, however, personal animus played an important part in shaping the president's ideology. Not until Biddle openly allied himself with Jackson's principal antagonists in Congress, Henry

Clay and Daniel Webster, did the president decide to crush the bank. When Biddle applied for a renewal of the bank's charter in 1832, four years before it was due to expire, the stage was set for a confrontation between pro-bank and anti-bank forces. In the battle that ensued on Capitol Hill, even some of Jackson's most stalwart supporters broke rank with the administration. Congress voted to extend the institution's charter, but in a bold and unprecedented act of executive authority, Jackson vetoed the bill on constitutional grounds, ignoring an earlier decision by the Supreme Court, which had ruled in the bank's favor. In Jackson's mind the bank war was no longer a contest between the advocates of a sound currency and the champions of unrestricted economic growth, but a titanic struggle between "the money power" and the people.

Jackson's opposition to the bank became the central issue of the 1832 presidential campaign. While the complex debate over federal fiscal policy may have been of little interest to many voters, the Jacksonian anti-bank message appealed to their emotions, playing skillfully on the fears of the electorate by portraying the B.U.S. as a sinister conspiracy bent on destroying the livelihood of the "common man." The Jacksonians staged huge rallies and parades to draw legions of voters to the polls, giving the president a comfortable victory over his long-time nemesis, Henry Clay. Interpreting his victory as a mandate for his policies, Jackson proceeded to take steps to sever the federal government's relationship with the bank when Congress convened after the election.

As one of Jackson's ablest floor managers in the House, Polk was taken off the Foreign Relations Committee and reassigned to Ways and Means, where he could be of greater service to the administration. As a member of the most important committee in the House, Polk would be expected to play a prominent role in the writing of a new compromise tariff bill and provide key support for Jackson's campaign against the B.U.S. Though he must have been gratified with this show of confidence in his abilities, Polk must also have known that the assignment was fraught with political risk. Democrats troubled by the administration's crusade to bring down the bank were reluctant to hazard an open breach with the "Old Hero," but they would not hesitate to direct their fire at Jackson's little-known lieutenant in the House. Polk had charted a safe course up to this point in his political career; now, for the first time, he would be a lightning rod for controversy.

Shortly after the legislative session opened, Jackson launched the next phase of his offensive against the bank. In his annual message, the president questioned the institution's solvency and called on Congress to determine whether it was still a safe depository for federal funds. The Ways and Means Committee conducted an investigation to look into the president's allegations, but its findings were a foregone conclusion: unwilling to incur the wrath of powerful commercial interests at home, a majority of the committee's members found no evidence of mismanagement.

Polk disagreed. Faithfully towing the administration line, the Tennessee congressman drafted the committee's minority report, which contained a detailed indictment of the bank. While stopping short of accusing the institution of violating its federal charter, the document was unsparingly critical of Nicholas Biddle, whom it accused of misrepresenting the bank's activities. The Tennessee congressman was particularly troubled by the recent revelation that the bank had been unable to cover a sudden and unexpected withdrawal of funds by the federal government. To meet its obligations, Biddle had dispatched a "secret agent" to London in 1832 to negotiate a special loan with a British banking house, a transaction made without the knowledge of the Treasury Department. The bank's efforts to conceal this information from the government warranted an "impartial and thorough examination of the books and affairs" of the institution, Polk argued. Any attempt by Biddle's friends in the House "to whitewash the bank," he warned, would not succeed.

When the session ended Polk returned to Tennessee to campaign for reelection, where he found that his position on the bank had earned him the enmity of many business leaders. Polk had run unopposed in his last two congressional races, but in 1833 he faced two challengers for his seat, who suspected that the Jackson ally might now be vulnerable on the bank issue. Adding to Polk's reelection worries, the rapid rise in the state's population had recently reduced his congressional district from four counties to two. Though Polk could still count on solid support in Maury, his anti-bank views had not met with widespread approval in neighboring Bedford County, the home and political stronghold of one of his campaign opponents.

The greatest threat to Polk's reelection came from outside his own district. As author of the Ways and Means Committee's minority report on the B.U.S., Polk was targeted for defeat by Biddle and his supporters, who attempted to manipulate public opinion on the bank's behalf. The *National Intelligencer,* the opposition newspaper in Washington, D.C., issued a special edition assailing the bank's detractors, devoting particular attention to the congressman from Middle Tennessee. Thousands of copies were printed and circulated throughout the state by the Nashville *Banner,* a local anti-Jackson journal. Outraged by "this insidious attempt on the part of the bank to interfere in the elections in this quarter," Polk was now more convinced than ever that the institution represented a corrupting influence, not only over the nation's economic affairs but over its elected officials and the press. For all his self-righteous indignation, however, the incumbent managed to overlook the fact that the Jacksonians' own news organ, the Washington *Globe,* had also flooded the country with copies of extra editions in an attempt to mobilize public opinion on its behalf.

Throughout the summer, Polk could be found everywhere his constituents gathered in large numbers. Few events provided a better opportunity to woo the voters than the religious revival, and it was at one of these camp meetings outside Columbia that he chanced to hear a sermon by John B. McFerrin, a young Methodist circuit rider. McFerrin's sermon made a profound impression on Polk, who went away from the revival with an appreciation for Wesleyan doctrine that would never leave him. In deference to his wife's devout Calvinism he did not formally join the church at this time, and continued to accompany Sarah to Presbyterian services every Sunday. On those occasions when she was unable to attend, however, he could usually be found worshiping with a Methodist congregation.

Methodism must have appealed to Polk for a number of reasons. In recent years it had become the fastest growing denomination in the state, drawing large numbers of Scots-Irish settlers away from Presbyterianism, which had been reluctant to embrace the democratic trends that were reshaping religious worship just as they were transforming other aspects of American life. Orthodox Presbyterians frowned on the ministry of untrained lay preachers and the undignified religious fervor of Baptist and Methodist revival meetings, clinging to the belief that only a predestined few would achieve salvation. Methodists rejected such doctrinal elitism, maintaining that Christ died for all men, a view that must have held a strong attraction for the earnest Jacksonian. Finally, the fact that Calvinist doctrine had long been a source of tension in Polk's own household, his father and grandfather having butted heads with local Presbyterian clergymen, may also have contributed to his preference for Methodism.

Despite his newfound religious beliefs, Polk never managed to break entirely free of the Calvinist tenets he had imbibed from his mother at an early age. While Polk may have accepted in principle the Methodist dogma that all men were capable of achieving God's grace, his own view of human nature was generally an unfavorable one. A man of stiff-necked moral rectitude, Polk felt that few could measure up to his own exacting standards of self-discipline, probity, and personal responsibility. Despite such contradictions, Polk's religious views were as much a part of his make-up as the ideology of republicanism. Together they formed a personal credo that governed Polk's every thought and action, both as a private citizen and public servant.

In the August election, Polk weathered his first serious challenge to his political career with remarkable ease, receiving more than twice the number of votes of his two rivals combined. By the fall he was back in the nation's capital, ready to aid the administration in what would prove to be the final round of its struggle against the Bank of the United States. In view of his stalwart support of Jackson's policy in the last session, the Tennessee congressman was promoted by the Democratic party leadership to chairman of the Ways and Means Committee. Polk's role would be crucial, for dissent within the party ranks over the bank issue seemed to be growing, so much so that the administration feared there might be enough pro-bank members of the new Congress to defy Jackson and grant Biddle an entirely new charter.

The president's veto and subsequent victory at the polls notwithstanding, the bank continued to conduct business more or less as usual, its contract having not yet expired. "The hydra of corruption is only *scotched,* not *dead,*" Jackson raged in a letter to Polk. Determined to bring down the bank without further delay, Jackson sought to strike at the very source of Biddle's financial power by removing the federal deposits from the bank. Jackson had already replaced one secretary of the Treasury, Louis McLane, who had advised a cautious policy toward the bank; he now fired a second, William Duane, when Duane balked at removal, and replaced him with Attorney General Roger B. Taney. Taney ordered that henceforth federal revenues would be deposited at selected state banks, and that existing deposits would slowly be withdrawn from the B.U.S. as needed to meet the expenditures of the federal government.

As the bank's currency reserves dwindled, Biddle was forced to call in outstanding loans, thus causing a severe shortage of credit. The president of the bank attempted to use the crisis to his advantage, calling in more loans than the emergency required in a last-ditch effort to exert pressure on Jackson to approve a new charter. Businessmen appealed to the White House to return the federal deposits to the B.U.S., but Jackson remained unmoved. "Biddle's Panic" ultimately backfired, leading many Americans to agree with Jackson that the bank did indeed exercise an unhealthy degree of control over the nation's economy.

At the height of the crisis, Polk rose on the floor of the House on December 30, 1833, to speak on behalf of the administration's anti-bank policy. Offering a point-by-point rebuttal of the charges of executive tyranny that the president's enemies had made against him, the chairman of the Ways and Means Committee defended Jackson's right to veto the recharter bill, remove intractable cabinet members, and withdraw federal deposits. Rather, Polk declared, the Bank of the United States had acted in a despotic manner, pointing to the existing financial emergency and Biddle's attempts to influence the political debate as proof positive of the institution's abuse of power.

Resuming his speech on January 2, Polk denounced the B.U.S. as "a great aristocracy of money" which, if allowed to continue unchecked, would have the power to control, and thus subvert, the nation's political institutions. If the bank enjoyed such formidable influence now, when forced to deal with an administration determined to curtail its power, Polk asked, "What would it be in the hands of corrupt men, at the head of affairs, whom it would prostitute itself to serve, and to whom it could bend to its own purposes?" Should the bank be granted a new charter to continue for another 20 years it would become "the veriest despot that ever ruled over any land," Polk declared. "The Bank of the United States has set itself up as a great irresponsible rival power of the government," he concluded. "The question is in fact whether we shall have the Republic without the Bank, or the Bank without the Republic."

Such hyperbole was not empty political rhetoric; like his mentor in the White House, Polk truly believed that a sinister conspiracy was afoot to undermine the nation's republican institutions. Since most members of the House had long since aligned themselves on one side of the bank issue or the other, Polk's speech probably won few converts. Nonetheless it was a succinct, cogent summary of the administration's position, so much so that the Democrats had it printed in pamphlet form and widely disseminated throughout the country. The speech enhanced Polk's stature in the Democratic party immensely. Now recognized as the undisputed leader of the Jackson forces in the House, Polk had become a figure of national prominence.

Biddle's desperate tactics could not save the bank, and when his charter with the federal government expired in 1836 the humbled financier was obliged to obtain a new charter with much-reduced powers from the state of Pennsylvania. The president had triumphed; the Bank of the United States was dead. As the self-appointed guardians of Thomas Jefferson's agrarian legacy, the Jacksonians believed they had saved the country from the tyranny of a privileged few. But dramatic as their victory seemed at the time, they had managed to kill only a symbol of the larger market forces they feared. The debate over the federal government's proper role in the nation's economic affairs would continue to rage in the years ahead. Andrew Jackson's controversial presidency nonetheless had lasting effects on American political life, shattering the broad republican consensus that had existed for more than a quarter of a century. Disturbed by the president's uncompromising and obdurate brand of leadership, some of his supporters now began to reassess their allegiances to the "Old Hero" and his political principles. Nowhere would the growing rift in the party ranks be more evident than in the birthplace of Jacksonian Democracy, Polk's home state of Tennessee.

3

The Shrine of Party

The president had won the bank war, but at a price to the Democracy that would only slowly become apparent. No other issue had so polarized the Jacksonians, although many disaffected Democrats remained at least nominally loyal to the party's standard bearer. The grumbling was loudest in the southern states, where support for Old Hickory had already ebbed in some quarters as a result of the nullification crisis. Southern Democrats had also been uniformly disappointed by Jackson's desire to groom New Yorker Martin Van Buren as his successor. With Jackson's retirement imminent, many southern Democrats now sensed that the time had come to distance themselves from the party leadership.

One of these restive Jacksonians was John Bell, an ambitious Tennessee congressman from Nashville. Though troubled by the administration's anti-bank policy, he had managed to tread carefully during Jackson's campaign against Nicholas Biddle and remained in the president's good graces. When rumors began to circulate in 1834 that the Speaker of the House planned to retire to accept a diplomatic appointment, Bell began to lobby for the coveted post.

Bell's campaign for the speakership put him on a collision course with another equally ambitious Tennessee congressman—the chairman of the Ways and Means Committee. Polk had been angling for the job for several months, dropping broad hints that he would put his name forward if called on to do so by the party leadership. "I think it a matter of great importance that the Speaker should be a man not only *true* in his politics," Polk wrote to a friend, "but one who has *always* been so, *never suspected,* and one who would give to the administration an honorable and hearty support." Polk believed he possessed these qualities; Bell, he was equally convinced, did not.

Though Polk was regarded as the administration candidate, Jackson remained ostensibly neutral in the contest, allowing a rift in the party ranks to develop that Bell was quick to exploit. The election for Speaker at the end of the first session of the Twenty-third Congress in June 1834 became a bitter, internecine struggle among various factions that left the party unable to unite on a candidate. Bell appealed to the anti-Jackson forces in the House for support, a breach of party discipline but a canny political maneuver that enabled him to win on the tenth ballot.

Stung by the defeat, Polk directed his friends in Tennessee to spread the word that the new Speaker had joined the opposition against Jackson. Despite his growing independence, Bell was not yet ready to cut his ties to the Democratic party, and when Congress adjourned he hurried home to reassure the voters of his district that he remained a committed Jacksonian. To marshal public support for their cause, both factions vied for control of the state's news organs. With the backing of Nashville's two newspapers, the Bell forces had the upper hand, effectively denying Polk a mouthpiece in Bell's congressional district. Polk and his supporters took steps to break their opponents' monopoly of information and political propaganda in this crucial part of the state by establishing an organ of their own, the Nashville *Union,* but in its early years the newspaper's meager financial resources and the chronic inebriation of its editor prevented it from exerting much influence.

Although Polk seemed to make little headway persuading the public that Bell had become a turncoat to the Jacksonian cause, he had more success convincing the one man who mattered most: Jackson himself. In the summer of 1834, the president had begun to suspect that the new Speaker did not share the administration's commitment to a hard money doctrine, noting in a letter to Van Buren: "if Mr. Bell does not come out clearly and distinctly against all national Banks he is politically destroyed." Bell refused to bend to the yoke of party discipline. In a speech delivered at Murfreesboro in October, he reportedly maintained that the administration's hard money policies were merely "an experiment," hardly the ringing endorsement the White House required. It was only a matter of time before Bell severed his connections completely with his erstwhile allies.

The rupture came the following year, when Jackson decided to endorse Martin Van Buren as the party's next presidential nominee. Unwilling to pledge their support to the New Yorker, Bell and a group of disgruntled Tennessee Democrats orchestrated a move to nominate favorite son Senator Hugh Lawson White for president in the 1836 election. White's candidacy proved highly embarrassing to the administration. Jackson's support in his home state remained broad and deep, but the Tennessee electorate was an independent-minded lot and could not be taken for granted. Old Hickory's endorsement notwithstanding, the urbane Van Buren elicited little enthusiasm among Tennessee's Democratic partisans who, as one New York politician put it, could never be loyal "to any man who did not squirt tobacco juice." The simmering feud between the Polk and Bell factions now erupted into open confrontation.

Polk's position was a decidedly awkward one. A long-time friend of White—they had once lived in the same Washington boardinghouse—he no doubt would have preferred him to Van Buren as the presidential nominee. Polk was also very much aware of the tremendous support for White's candidacy in his own congressional district. Even so, he could not be a part of any attempt to subvert the party's choice of nominee; torn between his friendship for White and his loyalty to Jackson, Polk never hesitated to choose the latter.

With Bell leading the movement to promote White's presidential bid, there could no longer be any question that the Speaker of the House had gone over to the opposition. Thus when the Twenty-fourth Congress convened in December 1835, the Democratic majority in the House moved quickly to undo the mistake it had made in choosing Bell as Speaker. Polk was widely viewed as the rightful candidate to unseat him, having been the party's second choice for the job one year earlier. Polk had, moreover, bolstered his reputation as a loyal party man by his refusal to be swept up in the groundswell for White in his home state. This time, the outcome was never in doubt. Backed by a solid Jackson majority, Polk won the post on the first ballot by a decisive 132 to 84 vote.

The rebellion in the ranks of the Tennessee Democracy was part of a much broader, nationwide realignment in American politics. In opposition to the party of Andrew Jackson, a new political organization emerged, which came to be known as the Whig party. Its moniker recalled the patriotism of the Revolutionary War to distinguish itself from the autocratic "King Andrew" and his followers. In the early stages of its development, the Whig party represented a loose coalition of political blocs united only by their opposition to Jackson and his successors. Many states' rights southerners bolted the Democratic party with

John C. Calhoun to protest Jackson's "executive usurpa-tion," but they had little in common with Whig national-ists such as Henry Clay and John Quincy Adams. As they eventually began to drift back into the Democratic fold, a distinct Whig ideology began to take shape. Whereas the Democrats tended to be fearful of rapid economic growth and the dislocating social changes that it engendered, the Whigs embraced the market revolution. Accordingly, the Whigs were inclined to be more supportive of an active government to stimulate the economy, while the Democrats adhered to strict constructionist principles, believing that the Constitution of 1787 had properly and clearly delin-eated the relationship between federal and state power.

The composition of the two parties reflected these dif-ferent views. Urban laborers and farmers adversely af-fected by the larger, increasingly competitive marketplace tended to vote Democratic. Whigs, who could not exist as a viable mass-based party without working-class support, appealed to those who benefited from industrial and com-mercial growth. While both parties drew their leaders from the ranks of community elites, Democratic party bosses tended to be provincial; Whig leaders, on the other hand, often hailed from commercial centers and enjoyed close ties with the local business community. In Tennessee, for example, Polk and other key Democrats were small-town lawyers and prosperous planters, whereas John Bell and Hugh Lawson White were well connected with Nashville's banking and mercantile interests.

Economic issues, however, were but one determinant of party affiliation. The two parties played a major role in providing opportunities for social interaction, and an in-dividual's voting preferences were very often shaped by those held by his family, friends, and neighbors. Militia units, fraternal brotherhoods, and volunteer fire depart-ments were organized along party lines—their officers elected by the rank and file according to their status within the state party hierarchy. In northeastern American cities, religious persuasion and ethnic origin were also part of the calculus of party membership. Thus party loyalties were based on a complex matrix of relationships and issues that defied simple socioeconomic classifications.

Once party allegiances had been established, they were not easily changed. Victories at the polls hinged less on the undecided vote than on the ability of the two organizations to get out their partisans at election time. Consequently, both parties placed a greater emphasis on electioneering than ideology, on the personalities of office-seekers rather than public policy. Mass rallies in the form of torchlight parades, barbecues, and bonfires were held in towns and cities across the country. Eastern wage laborers, western hardscrabble farmers, and southern planters all participated in the pageantry of American politics. In this way, the two-party system helped to forge the bonds of a popular mass culture.

James K. Polk was well suited temperamentally and intellectually to the new political order. Priding himself on his fixed principles, the Speaker of the House remained true to the Jacksonian creed, hewing the party line faithfully on such issues as the bank, the tariff, and internal improvements. The Whigs, he believed, with simple but unwavering conviction, were the ideological descendants of Alexander Hamilton and the Federalist party; only Democrats could claim to be the disciples of the true faith, Jeffersonian republicanism. In an age in which millions of Americans worshiped at the "shrine of party," few were as devout as James K. Polk.

The Tennessee Democrat's partisan ardor stemmed in large part from the fact that the two-party system offered him the equilibrium and order that he found lacking in society at large. Like many white Americans during the

Jacksonian era, Polk applauded the new democratic culture, with its unlimited freedoms and seemingly boundless economic opportunities. At the same time, however, he felt ambivalent about some of its most significant consequences. The equality of condition that defined Jacksonian America had unleashed an acquisitive spirit, a restless striving unknown to earlier generations. The rampant self-interest of the marketplace was rapidly displacing the community values of Polk's arcadian world. Disturbed by his society's crass materialism and its unseemly displays of self-aggrandizement, Polk found refuge in his party allegiances.

But there was an element of hypocrisy in his puritanical disapproval of those dedicated to the pursuit of gain. Relentless in his quest for higher political office, the Tennessee congressman was driven by the same fierce ambition that he sanctimoniously condemned in others. Polk's partisan loyalties were no doubt deeply felt, but they also served an important function on a purely personal level, so crucial to his own self-image, allowing him to piously assert that the welfare of the party always came before his own interests.

In keeping with his new position as Speaker, James and Sarah moved out of their boardinghouse and acquired more fashionable, commodious quarters at an establishment on Pennsylvania Avenue that catered to a clientele that included the Supreme Court justices and their wives. Their new lodgings had a parlor for entertaining and a dining room for meals, it being considered improper for the Speaker to dine with other members of the House. Although their religious convictions required them to decline invitations to some of the more popular social activities in the nation's capital—Sarah refused to attend horse races, for example—the Polks were active members of Washington society, frequently hosting receptions for members of Congress and visiting dignitaries.

The first session of the Twenty-fourth Congress was a tumultuous one for the new Speaker. It had become common practice in recent years for a handful of northern congressmen to present petitions from their antislavery constituents calling for the elimination of the slave trade and slavery in the nation's capital. Not surprisingly, this practice did not sit well with southern slaveholders. A few days into the session, James Hammond, a Calhoun Democrat from South Carolina, rose and demanded that the House receive no more antislavery petitions, which he regarded as an insult to the institutions of the South.

Anxious to avoid politicizing the slavery issue, most congressmen would have preferred to ignore the matter, but Hammond's motion involved a parliamentary question and therefore had to be addressed. Could the House refuse a petition that had been laid before it? Questions over the right of petition soon gave way, however, to a furious debate over slavery, with moderates of both sides drawn into the controversy. Always one to put party interests over sectional ones, Polk regarded northern and southern hard-liners as "fanatics" and "agitators." The Speaker struggled to maintain a semblance of order in the House while handing down rulings on procedural matters consistent with his strict constructionist principles. Near the close of the session, a committee created to study the issue presented the House with three resolutions carefully designed to win the support of moderates on both sides, although they failed to satisfy the extremists. One was the famous "gag rule," which called for all petitions relating to slavery or its abolition to be received by the House but then tabled without further discussion. The measures passed, but the gag rule would be reintroduced at the start of every session until antislavery congressmen led by John Quincy Adams managed to rescind it eight years later.

Polk's ongoing feud with the Bell faction made his first session as Speaker even more turbulent. From the floor, Bell and others defied Polk's authority at every turn, challenging his interpretation of the rules and harassing him with points of order. Some of Bell's more intemperate supporters in the Tennessee delegation assailed the Speaker in such bitterly personal terms that it was generally believed that they intended to provoke him into a duel. In firm control of his emotions and backed by a solid Jacksonian majority, Polk weathered these assaults against his position and his character. One New Hampshire Democrat noted approvingly that Polk "sustained himself as well as any man could have done, through the last long, laborious, fatiguing and stormy session. And notwithstanding the furious attacks upon him . . . embarrassing him with question after question of order, his equanimity was never disturbed . . . ."

In the presidential election of 1836, the newly formed Whig party nominated three candidates—Daniel Webster, Hugh Lawson White, and William Henry Harrison—in an attempt to deny the Democrats a majority of electoral college votes and thereby send the election to the House of Representatives. When Congress adjourned for the summer, Polk hurried back to Tennessee to urge voters to reject White's candidacy and stand by Van Buren, the party nominee. But his was a lone voice; even Democratic leaders who remained in the Jackson–Van Buren camp fell noticeably silent during the 1836 presidential race, hedging their bets should the Whigs win the election. Polk and a handful of Jackson stalwarts could only look on helplessly as local party leaders defected en masse to jump aboard the White bandwagon. For many Tennesseans in 1836, state loyalties proved stronger even than party ones, enabling White to outpoll Van Buren by 12,000 votes on election day. Nationwide, however, Democratic party ranks held firm, and Van Buren scored an easy victory against his three Whig challengers.

In the spring of 1837, Jackson handed the reins of government over to his hand-picked successor and made a triumphant return to Tennessee. The presidential entourage, which included James and Sarah Polk, was greeted by huge and adoring crowds at each stop along the way. At the string of banquets and parades held in Old Hickory's honor, the rancor that had hobbled the state's Democratic machinery seemed a thing of the past. But as recent events had amply demonstrated, Jackson's personal popularity could not be converted into political capital for a new generation of leaders. With the aging hero now in retirement, the Tennessee Democracy faced an uncertain future. In the euphoria that accompanied Jackson's return, none realized just how close the state's Democratic party was to complete collapse.

Even before Jackson arrived at the Hermitage, his plantation outside Nashville, eastern cities had begun to experience a rash of bank failures and factory closings. By mid-year, the entire nation was feeling the sting of a depression far worse than the one it had experienced in 1819. Angry voters blamed the economic distress on the Democrats, who countered by pointing out that the panic was an international phenomenon, the effects of which were being felt in Europe as well as in the United States. There could be no denying, however, that in crushing the B.U.S. Jackson had eliminated the only financial institution with the power to curb speculation by imposing credit controls on the American banking system. The effect of this and other Jacksonian fiscal policies had, at the very least, created a highly volatile economic climate that made the panic worse than it might otherwise have been.

The Panic of 1837 spelled disaster for the Democrats at the ballot box. Although the party managed to hold on to a thin majority in the House of Representatives, it suffered stunning defeats in the summer elections. In Tennessee, once an impregnable Democratic stronghold, the Jacksonians were in full retreat, with the Whigs winning the governor's office and ten of the state's 13 congressional seats (Polk, again running unopposed, was one of the Democratic survivors).

Polk was deeply troubled by the rout of the Democratic party in Tennessee, for his own fortunes and those of the state's party organization were closely intertwined. Though he professed to be motivated purely by the desire to serve his party faithfully, Polk's ambition remained undiminished. While the Speaker of the House at 41 years of age was too young to be considered presidential timber, he had reached the stage in his career where he could present himself as a legitimate candidate for the second spot on his party's ticket. There had long been talk of removing Vice-President Richard Johnson as Van Buren's running mate in the next election. A heavy drinker and the father of two children by a mulatto mistress, Johnson was viewed by many Democrats as a liability. To vie for such an honor, Polk would need the backing of a strong, well-organized political machine. Vice-presidential candidates were rarely selected on the basis of their personal charisma, but for their ability to deliver a major state's electoral college votes. As long as the Tennessee Democracy remained in eclipse, Polk's name would remain far down the list of likely candidates.

In the early months of 1838, demoralized Tennessee Democrats began to view Polk as the only man to reverse their party's sagging fortunes and urged him to resign his seat in Congress and run for governor. Polk initially expressed little interest in the idea, the governorship being a far less visible and less powerful position than the one he now held. But the longer Polk pondered the matter, the more attractive a gubernatorial bid became. If he could rescue Tennessee from the clutches of Whiggery, he could increase his stature in the Democratic party, and in the process develop the kind of strong, statewide political organization that might serve as a springboard for higher office. Polk's safest course was to remain in the House. But if the Whigs won a majority in the next election, he would have to content himself with a role as a leader of the opposition instead of Speaker. By the summer he had made up his mind: he would resign his seat in Congress after 14 years and run for governor. Publicly, Polk played the part of the reluctant candidate, who had consented to run only under pressure from his Democratic friends around the state. In fact, he had weighed his options carefully, ultimately deciding to take a bold but calculated risk that he hoped would lead to greater political rewards in the future.

The race was Polk's first statewide contest. Although popular in his own district, he was less well known in the commercial centers of East Tennessee and the poorer, western end of the state. Always a tireless campaigner, Polk resolved to win the election at the grassroots level. For four months during the spring and summer of 1839 he crisscrossed the state, giving speeches in every county. Polk returned to Columbia only twice during the campaign, stopping for a few hours of much-needed rest before hurrying off to another speaking engagement. The challenger was frequently joined on the campaign trail by Whig governor Newton Cannon. After riding on horseback all morning, the two candidates usually arrived at each campaign stop in the afternoon, then repaired to a grove on the outskirts of town accompanied by hundreds of local residents, where they squared off in a debate that might last up to six hours. Unable to keep up with Polk's grueling schedule, the lackluster Cannon fared poorly against his well-prepared and seemingly inexhaustible challenger. While Polk exhorted Tennesseans to return to the Democratic fold, in Columbia Sarah served as her husband's campaign manager, keeping him informed of the latest political news, handling his correspondence, and arranging to have fresh horses waiting for him at stops along the way. Polk seemed determined to reverse the fortunes of his party by dint of sheer perseverance.

In the end, his hard work paid off. The Democrat squeaked by the winner in a race that drew an unprecedented 89 percent of the electorate to the polls. In addition, the Democrats regained control of the state legislature and picked up three congressional seats. With republican humility, Polk downplayed his own role in the victory, stating simply, "I performed but the duty assigned me by my fellow citizens; a duty which I owed them, to the State, and to my principles." Democratic party leaders knew better, crediting Polk with having stemmed the Whig tide in Tennessee almost singlehandedly. Wrote New Hampshire senator Franklin Pierce in a letter of congratulation to the governor-elect: "this triumphant regeneration of Tennessee is regarded by both parties as of incalculable importance in settling the great political questions now pending before the nation . . . your name is upon the lips of all our friends coupled with expressions of applause & admiration." So far at least, Polk's strategy to position himself for the 1840 election was going according to plan.

The office Polk had labored so hard to gain allowed him but little control over public policy matters, the state constitution denying him even the power to veto bills passed by the General Assembly. Moreover, the small size of the state government afforded the incumbent only limited opportunities for patronage, inhibiting Polk's efforts to build a strong political machine. Thus the new governor's legislative program, which included reforms of the state banking system and internal improvements network, amounted to little more than suggestions to the General Assembly, which that body saw fit to disregard.

Despite a conspicuous lack of success in the legislative arena, Polk managed to bring the state's Democratic lawmakers dutifully into line behind his campaign for the vice-presidential nomination. Soon after Polk took the oath of office as governor in October 1839, the Tennessee General Assembly passed resolutions proposing Polk as Van Buren's running mate in the upcoming presidential race. Democratic party organs came out in favor of a Van Buren–Polk ticket, with each newspaper, in the custom of the day, announcing its preference on its masthead. Andrew Jackson, the party's patriarch, wrote to Van Buren and other prominent Democrats to lobby on Polk's behalf. Polk betrayed no hint of his ambitions, but behind the scenes he maintained an active correspondence with key party leaders, indicating that he would accept the second spot on the ticket if it were offered.

But Polk was not the only Democratic aspirant for the nomination. As the move to dump Johnson gathered momentum, several major factions of the party put their own candidates forward. Ironically, once it became clear that the selection of a new nominee would antagonize the other hopefuls and their partisans, support for Johnson as a compromise candidate began to revive. The various factions were still angling for position when the party held its convention in Baltimore in May. Lacking the support to win the nomination outright, Polk and other contenders for the second spot adopted a novel strategy; Van Buren's running mate, they argued, should not be chosen until after the election. In the event of a Democratic victory, the party could select a vice-presidential nominee during the balloting of the electoral college, thus avoiding a contentious and divisive fight on the eve of the campaign.

James K. Polk and Sarah Childress Polk strike an austere pose in this White House photograph. Sarah would outlive her husband by 42 years. Courtesy of the James K. Polk Memorial Assn., Columbia, TN.

Though Johnson proved to be the strongest candidate going into the convention, Polk's supporters successfully managed to play the spoilers' role, and the delegates adjourned without having selected a vice-presidential nominee. In so doing, the Polk forces kept their candidate's hopes for the vice-presidency alive, but their obstructionist tactics allowed the Johnson faction to claim that the will of the majority had been subverted by a small group of political operatives. Such charges were extremely discomforting for Polk, who had always professed to place the interests of his party above personal ambition. Accordingly, with support for Johnson on the rise, Polk issued a public letter three weeks after the Baltimore convention withdrawing his name from consideration.

Polk had little time to brood over his failure to win his party's nomination, for it soon became quite clear that Van Buren stood little chance of victory. Dubbed "Martin Van Ruin" by gleeful Whigs, the president was blamed for the worst depression in the nation's history. To make matters worse, the Democrats found that the grassroots electioneering tactics that had been their trademark and the key to their success in earlier campaigns were now being employed by the Whigs with similar results. Focusing on image-making rather than issues, the Whigs drew on the very themes that had once attracted legions of voters to the party of Andrew Jackson. Adopting no platform, the party nominated the aging veteran of the Battle of Tippecanoe, William Henry Harrison. To further bolster his popular appeal, the Whigs cynically touted their candidate as a yeoman farmer of humble origins, ignoring the fact that Harrison was a scion of one of Virginia's most aristocratic families. In an election of symbols and slogans, notable more for its carnival-like atmosphere than its discussion of weighty political questions, the Whigs rolled to victory in 1840 with their "Log Cabin and Hard Cider" campaign.

The following year, Tennessee Whigs had the opportunity to demonstrate their new-found mastery of these campaign techniques in the race for governor. Abandoning the somewhat lethargic Cannon, the party chose a homespun candidate with the "common touch" to run against Polk, 31-year-old state representative James "Lean Jimmy" Jones. In the summer of 1841 the two men took to the hustings. Polk, who had known nothing but success on the campaign trail, spoke to the issues in his earnest and dignified manner, sometimes injecting a note of humor in the form of an anecdote or two. In the wake of the boisterous presidential election, however, voters had come to expect more entertaining political fare. Jones offered the public what it wanted. Thin as a rail and dressed like a rube, the Whig challenger cultivated a comical appearance, which he combined with a folksy sense of humor. Jones became an instant hit with the voters, who preferred his story-telling to Polk's long-winded and carefully reasoned arguments on such issues as the national bank and the tariff. As a result, Tennesseans went to the polls and handed Polk his first defeat for public office.

Politics was too much a part of Polk's make-up for the ex-governor to consider retirement from public life. He remained the undisputed leader of the Democratic forces in the state, and the chance to run again as his party's candidate for governor was his for the asking. Though disappointed by the loss, he could take heart from the fact that the Whig coalition was already showing signs of disintegrating. William Henry Harrison had died of pneumonia one month after taking the oath of office. He was succeeded by Vice-President John Tyler, a Virginian of strong states' rights views, who proceeded to infuriate Whig nationalists by using his veto pen to block much of their economic agenda. With the Whigs rent by internal discord, Democrats across the country looked to the future with optimism, confident that their exile would be short-lived.

Continuing to regard the governorship as a stepping stone to higher office, Polk declared his intention to run again in 1843. As before, Polk aimed to reestablish the supremacy of the Democratic party in his home state, so that he might yet again emerge as a contender for the second spot on the national ticket. In his mind, the voters had been temporarily gulled by the opposition's campaign hoopla and the low comedy of "Lean Jimmy" Jones. Polk's Jeffersonian faith in their good sense remained undiminished, however, for he continued to believe that "the public mind, if sufficient time be given, will invariably arrive at correct results." Once the electorate realized its mistake, Tennessee would return to its rightful place in the Democratic column.

The speaking schedule for Polk and Jones was even more arduous than it had been two years earlier. For five months Polk canvassed the state, delivering more than 90 speeches. From their home in Columbia Sarah reprised her role as unofficial campaign manager, keeping Polk abreast of political developments in Middle Tennessee. Although she had become accustomed to long separations from her husband, the 1843 gubernatorial race was a trying experience for Sarah, who worried about the effects the campaign would have on his health. "I never wanted to see you more in my life than now," she wrote to him in early May. Polk urged her not to become despondent. "You must cheer up," he told her on June 9. "It is now but 7 weeks until the election. The worst of the canvass is over." One week later he wrote: "it distresses me that you are in such low spirits. If I could be with you, you know I would be."

Convinced that the voters had tired of Jones's antics, Polk went on the offensive, using all his formidable skill as a debater to attack the Whig program. While Polk sought to sway the voters with his command of the issues, Jones relied once again on his ready wit to blunt his challenger's sharpest arguments. Polk attempted to make an issue of the governor's open support of Henry Clay, the Whig party's likely standard bearer in 1844, but the Kentuckian was no longer the hated political figure he had once been. In the wake of the Panic of 1837, Clay's pro-bank policies had an undeniable appeal for some voters, while the familiar charge that he had conspired 18 years earlier to rob Andrew Jackson of the presidency now failed to elicit much public outrage.

Nonetheless, Polk continued to receive encouraging reports from Democratic partisans around the state as the August election approached. "Never have I seen the democrats in better spirits," one state legislator wrote the gubernatorial candidate in mid-July. Reported another hopeful political ally from Knoxville on the eve of the election: "we are making great inroads upon the Whigs." From Polk's vantage point, all signs seemed to augur well for a Democratic victory. Weary but confident, the candidate rode back to Columbia to await the outcome.

As the election returns came in, it became clear that the Democrats' optimism had been groundless. Indeed, for Polk and his supporters the results were nothing less than catastrophic; Jones won a second term by an even bigger margin than in the previous election, and the Whigs swept both houses of the General Assembly. Nashville, a Polk ally groaned when he learned of the results, had become "a political Sodom and Gomorrah of Whiggery." Across the state, the Jacksonians had been completely routed.

The defeat was the darkest moment of Polk's career. He had staked his entire political future on a quest to rescue Tennessee from the Whigs and had failed utterly. Worse, the defeat represented a frontal assault against Polk's most cherished ideals. As a staunch republican, he had never questioned the people's sound judgment, but twice he had appealed to their reason and been rebuffed; it was enough to shake his faith in the very idea of popular sovereignty. As a committed Democrat, he had remained steadfast in his loyalty to the party's leaders and its principles. But while he claimed to hold duty above personal ambition, the truth of the matter was that he had expected some reward for his services. None had supported the party more loyally, and it had availed him nothing.

Across the country, Democratic leaders who once considered Polk a front-runner in the vice-presidential sweepstakes now interpreted the election results in Tennessee as his political obituary. If Polk could not build a successful party organization in the state that had given birth to Jacksonian Democracy, he could hardly be the right man to help lead the Democrats to victory in a national election. With the party convention only a few months away, James K. Polk's political career appeared to have reached a dead end.

4

"The Most Available Man"

The election year of 1844 promised to hold few surprises. The Whigs, having expelled President Tyler from the party ranks for his opposition to their legislative program, were ready to unite behind long-time standard-bearer Henry Clay. By the summer of 1842, most of the Whig newspapers in the country had come out for the Kentuckian. The Democrats also appeared ready to field their most prominent party leader. Martin Van Buren, a veteran of the last two presidential campaigns, remained the overwhelming choice to head the party in 1844. Long before the two parties were scheduled to hold their national conventions to choose their presidential nominees, a race between Henry Clay and Martin Van Buren appeared to be a foregone conclusion.

From his home in Columbia, Polk took stock of the national political scene and surveyed the damage his defeat in the governor's race had done to his career. Bleak as the outlook seemed, Polk could take heart from the fact that if Van Buren won the nomination as expected, the party would probably choose a vice-presidential nominee from the South or Southwest to give the ticket regional balance. Although the Van Burenites had scrupulously avoided stating their choice for the second spot on the ticket, their dislike of perennial candidate Richard Johnson was well known. Polk's able lieutenant, Tennessee congressman Cave Johnson, enjoyed strong ties with the Van Buren men in Washington, and could be counted on to advance his friend's candidacy at every opportunity in the next session of Congress. Polk's political fortunes also received a much-needed boost from Andrew Jackson, who had not forgotten his protegé's yeoman service on behalf of the Democratic party over the years and did not desert him now in his hour of need. At the Hermitage, the ailing ex-president mustered what little strength he had left to scrawl letters to Van Buren and others, urging them to look to Polk as the only candidate who could win Tennessee for the Democrats in 1844. With the fires of ambition burning within him as brightly as ever, Polk convinced himself that all was not lost.

As Polk set about to salvage his political career, he could ill afford to appear demoralized. Some Tennessee Democrats had begun to talk openly of a new direction and new leadership for the party in the wake of its defeat in August. With the state party convention scheduled for November, Polk moved aggressively to reassert his authority over the party machinery before a serious challenge to his leadership could materialize, relying on the statewide following that he had developed during three gubernatorial campaigns. "There must be an immediate and bold rally of our friends through the [Nashville] Union," Polk urged a close political ally a few days after his defeat. "Let them be urged to keep their armour on, and to fight on for principle." As for himself, the ex-governor declared, "my sword is still unsheathed. . . ." When the convention met in Nashville, Polk's friends dominated the proceedings, securing the election of Polk delegates to the national convention in Baltimore and passing a resolution endorsing him for vice-president.

Polk appeared in control of his state's party apparatus— a vital first step forward in his comeback bid. Across the country, however, his stock had depreciated considerably since his gubernatorial defeat, and Democratic party conventions in other states gave his candidacy little notice. Richard Johnson seemed to have the inside track in the race for the nomination, while Alabama senator William King was also considered a contender for the second spot on the ticket. When Johnson picked up the key endorsement from the state organization in Ohio, King withdrew from the race. Although Polk refused to do likewise, Johnson's nomination seemed all but certain.

As the national convention drew nearer, it became apparent to astute political observers that Van Buren's road to the nomination was not so straight nor so smooth as had once been supposed. The New Yorker's support was wide but not deep; many partisans had lined up behind him more out of habit than genuine enthusiasm for his candidacy. He had been soundly beaten four years earlier, and for many Americans his administration would be remembered as an era of despair and privation. Most important, rising sectional tensions were making it extremely difficult for Van Buren to shore up his support in the South, where he was traditionally weak. In the steadily industrializing North, particularly in New York and Pennsylvania, Van Buren Democrats were unable to join with their southern brethren in denouncing Whig protectionist tariff policies. The slavery issue was also becoming an ever more divisive problem. Southern Democrats were enraged when some northern members of their party joined antislavery Whigs in the last session of Congress in an unsuccessful attempt to repeal the gag rule.

More than any other single issue, the question of Texas annexation had strained relations between the northern and southern wings of the party to the breaking point. After winning their independence from Mexico in 1836, Texans had voted overwhelmingly in favor of joining the United

States, but the Jackson administration, fearful that annexation might embroil the country in a war with Mexico, declined to accept the offer. Left to its own devices, Texas had established itself as a separate republic, although many of its citizens continued to hope that the United States would admit the fledgling nation at some future date. Meanwhile, opposition to annexation continued to grow in the Northeast, which was determined to prevent so vast an addition to the slave empire.

The Texas question lay dormant until 1843, when President Tyler, looking for an issue that might enable him to salvage his political fortunes, committed his administration to the annexation of the Lone Star republic. Tyler had become increasingly concerned about the close relationship that British diplomats enjoyed with Texas leaders. Such a bold initiative, he believed, would enable him to win not only the support of southern Whigs and Democrats, but all Americans who opposed British meddling in North America. Enlisting the aid of John C. Calhoun, who agreed to serve as secretary of state, the administration drafted a treaty of annexation with Texas diplomats after months of negotiations. Calhoun proved to be an unfortunate choice for the delicate task, roiling the already troubled political waters by promoting the measure as one vital only to southern interests. In the spring of 1844, the administration sent the treaty on to the Senate for ratification, thus forcing the two parties to address the issue on the eve of the campaign.

On April 27, a letter appeared in the *Globe,* Washington's Democratic news organ, which dramatically changed the course of the presidential contest. Anxious to defuse an explosive issue before it could do irreparable damage to the party, Martin Van Buren went on record to oppose Tyler's Texas treaty (a similar policy statement issued by presidential candidate Henry Clay appeared in the Whig

National Intelligencer the same day). Van Buren did not rule out the possibility of annexation, provided that Mexico could be induced to accept the loss of its former province. Ever cautious and sensitive to the interests of the southern wing of the party, Van Buren no doubt intended the letter to cement support for his candidacy. But for once the "Little Magician" had sorely misjudged the way the political winds were blowing. Southern Democrats wanted immediate annexation, not the promise of it at some later date. Many Democratic leaders now vowed to have nothing further to do with the party's long-time standard bearer.

Polk's supporters were thrown into a panic by these sudden developments. Their entire strategy for the upcoming convention was based on the assumption that Van Buren would be the party nominee. Washington was rife with rumors that if the Democrats failed to nominate a pro-Texas candidate, southern extremists would bolt the party and hold a convention of their own. John C. Calhoun, whose states rights, pro-slavery views made him anathema to many Democrats in the northern states, remained a strong favorite of the Deep South. With the Democrats hopelessly fractured along regional lines, the party's prospects of defeating a united Whig party in the fall seemed dim indeed.

Two weeks before the Baltimore convention, Polk received a summons from the Hermitage. Still a figure to be reckoned with in the Democratic party, Andrew Jackson believed there was only one way to solve the crisis. A fervent expansionist, he was convinced that Van Buren's letter had been "a fatal error." To bring the party together, a southwestern, pro-annexation candidate was needed at the head of the ticket. Polk, Jackson said, was "the most available man."

Polk was flattered but astonished. "I have never aspired so high," he wrote to his trusted lieutenant Cave Johnson.

Any attempt to place his name in nomination at the head of the ticket would surely be "utterly abortive." Polk's self-effacing estimate of his qualifications for the office, however, was short-lived. A letter to Johnson written two days later indicated that he had come around to Old Hickory's way of thinking on the matter. Should Van Buren fail to win the nomination in Baltimore, the Tennessee delegation should feel free to submit his name as a compromise candidate.

Far removed from center stage, both Andrew Jackson and his protegé seemed woefully out of touch with political reality. Although anything was possible given the volatile situation, the Tennessean lacked the public stature to be taken seriously as a candidate for the nation's highest office. Polk's lieutenants were too busy trying to salvage their candidate's vice-presidential chances to give much thought to so fanciful a notion as a presidential bid. Disheartened by the internecine strife on the eve of the convention, an unhappy Gideon Pillow, head of the Tennessee delegation, wrote to Polk, "You may consider every thing, even the fate of the party, as at *sea.*"

Pillow was not the only Democrat who worried that the party was foundering amid the tempest caused by Van Buren's April letter. Robert J. Walker, a Pennsylvania-born Mississippi senator, believed the time had come to chart a new course for the party and throw the old leadership overboard. A diminutive man with a high-pitched voice and a talent for political intrigue, Walker was of the opinion that the Democracy needed a new agenda that would capture the imagination of the American people. Frustrated by partisan bickering over sectional issues, he hoped to unite the Democracy under the banner of militant expansionism.

While the Van Buren and Calhoun factions eyed each other suspiciously, Walker was quietly recruiting insurgents from both camps who shared his vision of an imperial destiny for the United States. Two months earlier, Walker had laid the groundwork for his new crusade with the publication of a sensational manifesto, the *Letter . . . Relative to the Annexation of Texas*. Eschewing Calhoun's narrow-minded appeals to regional pride, Walker argued that annexation would be an economic boon to all sections and interest groups. Particularly startling was Walker's assertion that the annexation of Texas would actually alleviate sectional discord over the slavery issue. Speaking to the racist fears of both regions as only a northern-bred, southern politician could, Walker offered the ingenious argument that new western lands would serve as a safety valve for the Deep South's surplus slave population, thereby quieting northern fears of a black migration into the free soil states. Walker even predicted that free blacks would, over time, voluntarily migrate southward into Mexico, a process that would ultimately resolve the so-called "Negro problem" for anxious white Americans.

The Baltimore convention would provide the real test of Walker's growing influence. Intent on denying Van Buren the nomination, Walker and other expansionists favored Michigan senator Lewis Cass, who had come out strongly in support of Texas annexation. But the likelihood that they would be able to steal the nomination from the Democrats' long-time standard-bearer appeared remote. A majority of delegates had been pledged to Van Buren long before the New Yorker made public his controversial stand on the Texas question. A few of the more intractable southerners claimed that this pledge was no longer binding, but they remained in the minority. Despite their doubts about whether the New Yorker could win for them in November, most of the delegates felt dutybound to honor their commitment to support Van Buren on the first ballot. Thus in spite of the furor caused by their candidate's stand on Texas, the Van Burenites had reason for optimism as the convention approached. They were prepared for a fight, but confident about the outcome.

On May 27, 266 Democratic delegates assembled at the Odd Fellows' Hall in Baltimore. The Whigs had met in the city to nominate Henry Clay by acclamation a month earlier, adopting a platform that ignored the Texas question entirely. Any hopes that the Democrats would meet in a similar spirit of party harmony soon faded.

Quickly outmaneuvering the Van Burenites, the Walker faction secured the election of a convention chairman hostile to the New York delegation, then lobbied for a rules change requiring a two-thirds majority for nomination. Although the two-thirds rule had been followed in earlier conventions, the party's tradition of uniting behind its nominee made it a formality, and it had been abandoned in 1840.

The Walker faction's motion to change the nominating rules threw the convention into an uproar. Despite their strong delegate lead, the Van Burenites could not command a two-thirds majority needed to win the nomination on the first ballot. If the rules change passed, pro-annexation delegates could honor their pledge to vote for Van Buren on the first ballot, knowing full well that he lacked the support to capture the nomination. Having fulfilled their obligations to the party leader, they could then cast about for a candidate more attuned to their expansionist agenda.

For two days the convention was rocked by furious and acrimonious debate over the proposed rules change. Benjamin Butler, the leader of the New York delegation, pleaded with the delegates to defeat the motion, while a gleeful Walker took the floor to taunt the Van Burenites for opposing it. When the votes were counted, the motion to adopt the two-thirds rule carried, with a large number of delegates committed to Van Buren voting for the measure. Some were disgruntled annexationists who no longer supported the New Yorker's candidacy. Others wanted the convention to agree on a nominee by a two-thirds majority in order to discourage the South from fielding its own candidate, thereby saving the party from almost certain defeat in the fall. Whatever their reasons, Walker had triumphed, effectively robbing Van Buren of the front-runner status he had enjoyed when the convention began.

As expected, Van Buren ran well ahead of other contenders on the first roll call, but 26 votes short of the necessary two-thirds majority. He continued to lead for the next three ballots, but with each vote Lewis Cass picked up strength. On the fifth ballot the Michigan senator emerged as the front-runner, but like Van Buren he could not muster enough votes to win the nomination. After seven inconclusive ballots and with no end to the deadlock in sight, the exhausted delegates adjourned for the evening.

Party leaders huddled well into the night to find some way out of the impasse. Seething with bitterness, the Van Burenites knew that Cass would continue to gain momentum when the delegates reconvened the next morning. Utterly opposed to the Michigan senator, they were determined to deny victory to the faction that had robbed them of the nomination. Clearly, in the interests of party unity, a compromise candidate was needed. George Bancroft, the leader of the Massachusetts delegation and a Van Buren supporter, suggested the leader of the Tennessee Democracy, James K. Polk.

Although Polk had not received a single vote in the first day of balloting, his candidacy had certain obvious advantages. Having taken an unequivocal stand in favor of annexation, he was acceptable to the expansionist wing of the party. Equally important, the Tennessean had played no part in the effort to sabotage Van Buren's candidacy and remained on good terms with the leaders of the New York delegation. Finally, Polk had received the blessing of Andrew Jackson, no small point in his favor among

Democratic stalwarts desperate for a candidate to return the party to its former glory.

That night Bancroft and Polk manager Gideon Pillow tried to sell the state delegations on the idea of offering Polk as a compromise candidate. With Bancroft's prodding, some of the Massachusetts and New Hampshire delegates agreed to swing their votes to Polk when the balloting resumed the next day. Pillow worked the southern delegations and managed to obtain the support of Alabama and Mississippi. The leader of the latter delegation, Robert J. Walker, felt no personal loyalty to Cass and was perfectly amenable to any nominee who supported annexation. The New York managers, not yet reconciled to defeat, favored withdrawing Van Buren and substituting a close ally of the ex-president, popular New York senator Silas Wright. Some doubted that Wright would accept the nomination, however, and when the delegation met the following morning it decided to abandon the idea. Thoroughly outmaneuvered, the Van Burenites seemed paralyzed by indecision, as the course of events now slipped completely beyond their control.

When the delegates were called to order on May 29, it became apparent that the supporters of Lewis Cass, known contemptuously as the "Jack Casses" by their opponents, had not been idle during the night. Kentucky's delegates, who had hitherto cast their ballots for favorite son Richard Johnson, now switched to Cass. But it was not enough. Cass still led after the eighth ballot, but his drive for the nomination had stalled; three states—Tennessee, Alabama, and Mississippi—abandoned the Michigan senator and went for Polk, who polled a distant but respectable third in the voting.

The sudden emergence of the Tennessean as a contender for the nomination created a buzz of excitement throughout the hall. State delegations caucused hurriedly to rethink their strategy as the balloting resumed for the ninth time.

The first states called declared for Polk. The momentum had clearly shifted to the convention's "dark horse" candidate.

At last, the New York delegation, the single largest bloc of votes, bowed to the inevitable. Benjamin Butler rose, and in a voice breaking with emotion withdrew Van Buren's name and threw his support to Polk. With that dramatic announcement, a loud cheer resounded throughout the hall. The deadlock was broken. Pandemonium broke loose as state after state now went for Polk. At the end of the balloting, the last remaining Cass delegates changed their votes to make the former governor of Tennessee the unanimous choice of the Democratic party. "I never saw such enthusiasm, such *exultation,* such *shouting for joy,*" a jubilant Gideon Pillow declared.

Hoping to conclude their convention on a note of party harmony, the delegates extended an olive branch to the Van Buren faction by nominating Silas Wright for vice-president. But the Van Burenites were not so easily mollified. From Washington, Wright promptly sent word by telegraph refusing the nomination. Wright harbored no ill feelings toward Polk personally, but he believed the convention had done Van Buren a grave injustice. He would do nothing to render aid to the faction that had robbed Van Buren of his rightful place at the head of the ticket.

Robert J. Walker, reveling in his new role as the party's kingmaker, now seized the opportunity to put forward former Pennsylvania senator George M. Dallas. A prominent Philadelphia attorney and the uncle of Walker's wife, Dallas had supported the party's position on Texas, and his close ties to business interests in his home state would help to quiet fears that a Polk administration would adopt a free-trade tariff.

That afternoon the delegates assembled again, this time to adopt a platform that the indefatigable Walker had drafted. The platform included the usual planks on behalf of limited government and a low tariff. Predictably, the party took a strong stand on Texas annexation, and in an effort to attract western voters to the expansionist cause called for the United States to establish its control over the entire Oregon territory, an area that it had claimed jointly with Great Britain for almost three decades.

Its business concluded, the convention broke up in an atmosphere of euphoria and relief. Only 24 hours earlier, the party had seemed on the verge of splintering apart. Almost miraculously, the crisis had been averted, and the turbulence of the past three days forgotten. But the appearance of unity was deceptive. Wright's decision to decline the second spot on the ticket revealed that the convention had only aggravated the animosities that beset the party. Van Buren's supporters would not soon forget their humiliation at Baltimore.

Blaming their misfortunes on a southern conspiracy, the Van Burenites missed the real significance of the convention. The South was indeed eager to jump aboard the Polk bandwagon, but the revolt within the ranks had not been engineered by slaveholding extremists. In 1844, Robert J. Walker's vision of a continental destiny for the United States seemed to offer to many Democrats a new direction for the party. No longer a corollary to the sectional debate, expansionism had now been thrust to the forefront of the American political agenda. Here at last was an issue that could ignite the passions of a broad range of interest groups—not only slave owners who wanted Texas, but midwesterners who demanded settlement of Oregon and New Englanders who craved new commercial markets. Both Van Buren and Calhoun would continue to command large and loyal followings, but their days as the party's prime movers had passed.

The Polk forces were not blind to the fact that the unexpected outcome in Baltimore had alienated many party leaders. Accordingly, in a letter formally accepting the nomination, their candidate made a remarkable promise: if elected, Polk vowed to serve only one term. The move was not an empty gesture to be retracted four years later. Genuinely distressed by the rancor that had so divided the party in recent years, Polk sought to unite all factions of the Democracy behind his candidacy. Those dissatisfied with the choice could pin their hopes on the next election.

The news of the Baltimore convention was received with disbelief among loyalists of both parties. Stunned Whigs were delighted with the Democratic ticket. Political contests, particularly at the national level, hinged on personalities and name recognition. Only elder statesmen and military heroes were deemed worthy of carrying a party's standard in a presidential race. The Democrats had defied convention by nominating two candidates largely unknown to the electorate. "Who is James K. Polk?" would become the derisive chant of the Whigs in the months ahead. Although Polk was by no means a nonentity, neither he nor his vice-presidential nominee held public office in 1844. Dallas had given so little thought to the possibility of being nominated for the vice-presidency that when a delegation awoke him in the middle of the night to inform him of the news, he feared there had been a death in his family.

One important item of business remained before Congress adjourned and the campaign season began in earnest—the Senate vote on Tyler's Texas treaty. Still smarting from their Baltimore defeat, Van Buren's supporters took no small amount of satisfaction in joining with the Whigs to defeat the measure in June. But the vote proved to be only a temporary setback rather than the death knell for annexation. Undaunted, Tyler promptly announced that he would try a different approach; in the next session of Congress he would present the issue again, this time as a joint resolution, which would require only a simple majority of both houses rather than the two-thirds majority needed for Senate ratification.

With the fate of annexation still uncertain, the issue took center stage in the presidential campaign. Still entertaining hopes of a second term, Tyler remained a candidate, although the Democrats' decision to abandon Van Buren in favor of a pro-annexation nominee had doomed whatever remote chance of victory the incumbent might have had in November. Realizing that his candidacy served no purpose other than to split the expansion vote, Tyler finally succumbed to Democratic pressure and withdrew from the race in August, consoling himself with the hope that he might yet be able to consummate his dream of annexing Texas before his term expired.

With the expansionists united behind a single candidate, Whig nominee Henry Clay found himself in an unenviable predicament. Sensing that he had misjudged the depth of public support for annexation, Clay began to qualify his earlier statements on the Texas question. In an effort to prevent a Democratic sweep of the South, the Whig nominee now averred that he favored annexation, but only if it could be achieved without a war with Mexico. The gambit backfired badly. Anti-slavery Whigs in key northern states were enraged, many of whom now bolted to the abolitionist Liberty party. The hapless Clay was compelled to issue yet another statement on the subject that, far from clarifying his position, only confused matters, leaving him vulnerable to charges of inconsistency and vacillation on the eve of the election.

From his home at Columbia, Polk remained aloof from the campaign fray. While the Democratic nominee maintained an active correspondence, coordinating strategy with party leaders across the country, he left the state organizations to present the Democratic message to the electorate.

Polk issued only one policy statement during the course of the campaign, clarifying his stand on the controversial tariff issue in a public letter to John Kane, a Pennsylvania manufacturer and associate of vice-presidential nominee Dallas. Taking a middle-of-the-road position designed to allay the fears of the business community, Polk declared his opposition to protectionism on principle, pledging instead his support for a tariff high enough to raise revenue for the federal government. For the most part, both sides managed to avoid the mudslinging characteristic of recent presidential campaigns. Polk's reputation for probity was so unimpeachable that Whig pundits were obliged to focus their attacks on his deceased grandfather, alleging that Ezekiel had been a Loyalist in the American Revolution, a charge the Democratic nominee vigorously denied.

The election returns came in slowly, since voting was scheduled on different days for many states, ranging from the first to the 12th of November. In Columbia, the Polks waited anxiously for the results. The early returns were promising, with the news that the Democrats had carried Pennsylvania. But the race remained close for several days, and it was not until the final votes had been tallied in New York that Polk's victory was assured. The election was one of the closest in history, with Polk receiving less than 40,000 votes more than Clay out of some 2,700,000 cast. In some states, the winner had been decided by razor-thin margins. Amid allegations of election fraud, Polk failed to carry Tennessee by a mere 123 votes, although he edged out his Whig opponent in enough key states to give him a solid 170 to 105 victory in the electoral college.

For all the furor over annexation, Texas had not been the only issue of the campaign. Polk's adroit handling of the tariff question had undoubtedly been a significant factor in his victory in Pennsylvania. The presidential contest was also affected in northern urban centers by the strident nativism and anti-Catholicism of local Whig candidates, which had prompted large numbers of immigrants to vote Democratic. Nonetheless, Clay's inept handling of the Texas issue cost him much-needed votes in New York state and turned out to be his greatest blunder of the campaign.

While Polk would not take the oath of office for four months, he was about to face one of the greatest trials of his career. The Democrats had emerged victorious from the presidential election, but by no means united. Before assuming leadership of the nation, Polk would first have to exert his control over a fractious party. To many Democrats, Polk remained very much an unknown quantity. For the Van Burenites, he would forever be regarded as a pretender to the Jackson throne. Even many Democrats who had been among the first to rally to Polk in Baltimore felt little personal loyalty to the president-elect. The prospect of winning federal patronage would, for the time being, keep these various factions in line, but Polk could not reward one wing of the party without inciting the jealousy of another. It remained to be seen whether the president-elect would be able to fuse these disparate elements into a viable political organization.

The selection of a cabinet would provide the first test of the new president's political skill. Much more than a list of advisers, Polk's cabinet appointees would be closely scrutinized by party leaders for clues as to which faction would enjoy the most access to the president in the new administration. Not only would the party's major power blocs insist on being represented in the six-member cabinet, but each would expect a position commensurate with its own perceived importance in the national Democratic organization.

Those factions that hoped to dominate the new president, however, did not know him. Stubborn and strong-willed by nature, Polk was determined to be the master of his own house. "I intend to be *myself* President of the U.S.,"

Polk confided to Cave Johnson shortly before the inaugural. At the same time, Polk was an old hand at the byzantine intrigue of party politics and well aware that he could not make his cabinet appointments without regard to the competing interests of his party. To offend one of them would be to court disaster before his administration had even begun.

In the weeks that followed the election, Polk devoted his energies almost exclusively to the extremely delicate task of appointing a six-member cabinet that would satisfy everyone. The president-elect did not want for advice; Polk was inundated by correspondence from Democrats from across the country urging him to consider certain party leaders for key cabinet positions. After consultation with Andrew Jackson, Polk and his lieutenants had by year's end narrowed the field of possible candidates and sent out feelers to ascertain the interest of some of them in prospective appointments. Owing to the slowness of the mails, Polk had still not decided on a final roster for his cabinet when he left Columbia for the nation's capital in late January. En route the president-elect made one final visit to the Hermitage to pay his respects to the man who had done so much to promote and guide his political career. Jackson would be dead four months later, comforted by the knowledge that "the Republic is safe," with his protegé at the helm.

The Polks arrived in Washington on February 13, 1845, where they moved into a suite of rooms at the Coleman Hotel. With two and a half weeks remaining before the inaugural, public interest in the president-elect's appointments had reached a fever pitch. A crowd of Democratic politicians hovered about the hotel, all anxious to gain the president-elect's ear before the final decisions on the cabinet were made.

For secretary of state, the most prestigious cabinet post, Polk had already made a tentative choice—the polished and urbane Pennsylvania senator James Buchanan. A rising star in the Democratic party, Buchanan would bring to the administration much-needed support in his home state, where manufacturing interests remained decidedly wary of Polk's views on a lower tariff. The appointment was bound to cause friction with Vice-President Dallas, who had in recent years been locked in an acrimonious struggle with Buchanan for control of the Pennsylvania Democracy. Buchanan's well-known presidential ambitions were also a concern. Polk had not forgotten how Calhoun and Van Buren had engaged in an unseemly scramble for position as the president's heir-apparent in the early days of the Jackson administration. Determined to keep his cabinet members focused on public policy rather than politicking, Polk decided to ask each appointee to pledge to forswear from seeking higher office while serving as a member of his administrative team. Buchanan's response was equivocal; the Pennsylvania senator refused to state if he would be a candidate for the presidency in 1848, but promised not to seek the office without Polk's permission. On the basis of this assurance, Polk invited Buchanan to join the cabinet as secretary of state.

By far the most nettlesome problem for Polk in the selection of a cabinet was his choice of a New Yorker. Although the Van Buren camp, still angry over its defeat in Baltimore, had mounted only a lukewarm campaign on behalf of the national ticket in the recent election, Polk could not afford to slight this all-important wing of the party. The president-elect knew that a prestigious cabinet appointment for one of their own would ensure the Van Burenites' support for his administration, but his efforts to give it to them soon ran aground. Having corresponded at length with Van Buren and his advisers since November and taken due note of their suggestions for suitable appointees, Polk offered cabinet-level posts to two of Van Buren's top lieutenants, Silas Wright and Benjamin Butler.

Both declined; Wright, having just been elected governor of New York, turned down the job of secretary of the Treasury, while Butler believed the proferred position of secretary of war beneath his stature in the party. With time running out to make his cabinet appointments before the inauguration, Polk asked William Marcy, a former governor of New York, to serve as secretary of war. Evidently, Polk hoped that Marcy would be acceptable to Van Buren, but in this he was mistaken. A pro-Texas expansionist, Marcy had recently broken with the Van Burenites. Instead of placating the party's most important faction, Polk had unwittingly alienated it still further.

To satisfy the South, Polk wished to bring Robert J. Walker into the cabinet, but in order to do so, John C. Calhoun, the region's preeminent public figure, would first have to be diplomatically persuaded to step aside. Although still involved in delicate negotiations with Texas, Calhoun solved this dilemma for the president-elect by offering to resign as secretary of state. Polk initially considered offering Walker the position of attorney general, but the Mississippi senator's friends believed the post to be unworthy of his talents. Under considerable pressure, not only from southerners but from the party's expansionists, Polk tapped Walker to serve as secretary of the Treasury. The appointment, of course, did not sit well with the Van Buren camp, who regarded Walker as the evil mastermind of the Baltimore convention. Nor was opposition to the mercurial Mississippian limited to the northern wing of the Democratic party. In a letter written two days before his death, Andrew Jackson warned Polk that Walker's financial difficulties and unsavory business connections made him unsuitable for such a post. But the debt the president-elect owed Walker needed to be repaid, and Polk stood firm in his decision.

The other three appointments were far less controversial. New Englander George Bancroft, who had placed

Polk's name in nomination in Baltimore, was named secretary of the navy. Rounding out the cabinet were two men well known to Polk. Tennessee congressman Cave Johnson, perhaps Polk's closest friend, accepted the job of postmaster general. John Y. Mason, a North Carolinian and college classmate of the president who had served as Tyler's secretary of the navy, was tapped to serve as attorney general.

Taken as a group, they were staunch Jacksonians, representing every major region of the country, who shared, to varying degrees, the president-elect's political views. Despite the best of intentions on Polk's part, however, his cabinet appointments left certain segments of the party disaffected. Dallas had privately confided to friends that he would resign if Buchanan received a cabinet appointment, and although he did not make good on this threat, his relations with the new president were strained from the beginning. Much more important, the Van Burenites, who made no effort to conceal their unhappiness with the appointments of Marcy and Walker, were now firmly convinced that Polk had fallen completely under the sway of their intraparty rivals.

In fairness to the president-elect, no Democratic leader, no matter how accommodating, could have satisfied all the competing factions of his party. The house that Jackson built had long dominated the American political landscape, but by 1845 it had fallen into disrepair. While internecine struggles over patronage contributed to its ramshackle appearance, its problems were fundamental rather than cosmetic. Straddling an ever-widening sectional fault line, this once imposing monument to party solidarity had been rocked by a series of tremors over Texas and slavery. It remained to be seen whether the new president-elect could repair the damage before the edifice became structurally unsound.

5

"I Am the Hardest Working Man in This Country"

While Polk scrambled to assemble a cabinet in the days before the inaugural, the scene on Capitol Hill was one of similarly hectic activity. As the legislative session drew to a close, the troublesome Texas issue remained a question in want of a solution. Supporters of annexation had not been idle since the November election. In his last months in office, lame duck chief executive John Tyler had pushed strenuously for a joint resolution calling for the immediate annexation of Texas. The measure passed the House of Representatives but encountered stiff opposition in the Senate, where support was strong for a proposal advanced by Democratic Missouri senator Thomas Hart Benton, who called for an entirely new treaty to be negotiated with Texas. In a last-ditch effort to clear the way for an annexation bill before Congress adjourned, Senator Robert J. Walker worked out a compromise that in effect combined both bills into one legislative package, giving the new president the option of choosing either plan once in office. Supporters of the Benton plan sounded out the president-elect on the matter and came away with the distinct impression that he favored their own alternative. Accordingly, the Missouri senator and his followers lined up behind the compromise bill, which Tyler signed three days before Polk took the oath of office.

There the matter should have rested until after the inauguration, but the outgoing Tyler had other plans. Although Congress had clearly intended that Polk decide which of the two proposals should be presented to Texas, Tyler did not want to be robbed of the chance to make annexation the crowning achievement of his administration. On his last night in office he dispatched a courier to Texas, offering to admit the Republic into the Union under the terms of the House plan. Tyler's unexpected maneuver was not irreversible. The president-elect could have recalled the courier after taking the oath of office. But like Tyler, Polk was anxious to annex Texas without further delay, and the House measure offered the surest and quickest means of doing so. If Polk had ever seriously considered the Benton alternative, he made no attempt to save it now and allowed Tyler's action to stand.

A steady rain was falling on March 4 when James K. Polk took the oath of office as the 11th president of the United States. In a firm, clear voice, the 49-year-old Polk—the youngest chief executive up to that time—delivered his inaugural address on the steps of the Capitol to "a large assemblage of umbrellas." Dwelling on the annexation of Texas more than any other subject, the new president issued a thinly veiled warning to Mexico not to disrupt the impending nuptials between the United States and the Texas Republic. They "are independent powers," Polk noted, "and foreign nations have no right to interfere with them or to take exceptions to their reunion." Polk also used his inaugural address to deliver a message to Great Britain on the subject of Oregon, asserting that the American title to the entire Pacific Northwest was "clear and unquestionable."

In the weeks that followed, the new president continued to keep silent on the subject of annexation; meanwhile, the Bentonians voted for Polk's cabinet appointments and in other ways dutifully toed the administration line. But as it slowly became apparent that the new president would not present the Benton alternative to the government of Texas after all, supporters of the measure accused Polk of acting in bad faith. Polk would later insist that he had never given the Benton men any reason to think that he was committed to their annexation plan, but the episode was more than a simple misunderstanding, for he had certainly encouraged them to believe otherwise.

During the next four years there would be many more occasions when critics of the president would point to his penchant for disingenuousness, if not outright deception. To his political enemies, the Tennessean exhibited a "trait of sly cunning which he thought shrewdness" that would ultimately earn him the unflattering sobriquet "Polk the Mendacious." Those close to the president generally took a kinder view, maintaining that Polk was by nature taciturn and self-contained, qualities which, they admitted, he often used to good advantage. George Bancroft could marvel at Polk's ability to keep "his mouth as effectively shut as any man I know." At the very least, the president was a man of dignified reserve who played his cards close to the vest, and in so doing often kept even his closest associates guessing as to his real intentions.

If Polk's methods at times seemed underhanded and devious, there could be no secret about the political principles that guided him. The Jacksonian gospel found its most ardent disciple in the new president. Like his mentor, Polk took the view that the president, as the only federal office-holder elected by all the people, was their true representative; a vigorous chief executive, he believed, was the most effective safeguard against the parochialism of the legislative branch. Andrew Jackson's influence could also be seen in the new administration's economic policies. Polk's campaign pledge to reduce the Whig tariff of

1842, and his opposition to a national bank and federally funded internal improvements, all stemmed from the conviction that the government had no constitutional authority to intervene in the nation's economic affairs. In foreign policy, Polk shared Jackson's strong suspicions that Great Britain represented the most serious threat to the nation's continental ambitions; at all hazards, the United States must check British designs wherever they appeared, in Texas, Oregon, and throughout the hemisphere.

At the outset of his administration Polk mapped a course using these political coordinates and never deviated from them. The president derived great strength from his unshakeable faith in Jacksonian precepts, which allowed him to focus his considerable energies on specific, clearly delineated objectives. Not given by nature to introspection, the president was a complete stranger to self-doubt, and was rarely dissuaded once he had made up his mind. Such ideological rigidity was not an unqualified asset, however. Polk would face a series of unique problems as the nation's chief executive that defied easy, ready-made solutions. His was a well-ordered but inelastic mind, uncluttered by abstractions and closed to new ideas.

Polk was as stiffly formal in his personal relations as he was dogmatic in his political views. The grim, humorless president had few close acquaintances and seemed most content when working alone at his desk, attending to official business. He had no hobbies or pastimes, no interests beyond the duties of his office. His reading material consisted entirely of government documents and the Scriptures. Provincial in outlook and tastes, Polk knew little of the world beyond rural Tennessee and showed no particular inclination to learn. Dressed in an unfashionably long black coat, its pockets bulging with letters, the president reminded naval explorer Charles Wilkes of a "penny postman" who "had little to converse about" besides politics.

He regarded the arts with disdain, becoming quite irritated when two American diplomats, during an informal meeting in his office, engaged in a spirited debate on the merits of a famous sculptor. Unacquainted with such matters, the president had nothing to contribute to the conversation and sat in silence.

To the puritanical Polk, even the most innocent diversions seemed a frivolous waste of time. When a juggler and magician performed at the White House, the president, whose mind was preoccupied with a growing crisis with Great Britain over the Oregon territory, found the show "innocent in itself, but I thought the time unprofitably spent." Even birthdays were occasions not for celebration but for sober-minded reflection. On his 53rd birthday, the president recorded the following melancholy entry in his diary: "I am solemnly impressed with the vanity and emptiness of worldly honours and worldly enjoyments, and of [the wisdom of] preparing for a future estate."

The president's passion for efficiency and order could be seen in his daily schedule at the White House. He began his day at sunrise with a walk around the White House grounds. After breakfast Polk opened his office to visitors—except on Tuesdays and Saturdays, when the cabinet was in session—during which time he made himself available to an unending stream of congressmen, official delegations, and private citizens. From noon until late afternoon he worked at his desk on official business. Since Congress allocated no funds for the president's staff—not until 1857 would it see fit to provide for an executive assistant—Polk paid for a private secretary, his nephew Joseph Knox Walker, out of his own pocket. Walker and his family occupied two rooms in the White House, and together the two men tried vainly to cope with the tremendous volume of paperwork and routine business that daily crossed the president's desk. On those occasions when Walker was away from his post, Polk was obliged to sign land patents and perform other menial duties himself. After dinner, the president took another walk or, on occasion, a horseback ride in the company of Cave Johnson or Judge Mason. Returning to his office, he continued to receive visitors well into the night, and yet still found time before retiring to keep a meticulous and detailed diary of the day's events.

Sundays represented the only interruption in Polk's grueling schedule. The first family usually spent the morning at church services, and the rest of the day quietly at home. The president ordered the White House steward to admit no visitors to the executive mansion, a rule that applied to congressional leaders as well as the general public. But affairs of state did not always respect the sabbath, and occasionally, during times of political crisis, Polk was obliged to break this rule.

Polk's managerial style also reflected his methodical, if rather inflexible personality. Under the new chief executive the policy-making process became systematized as never before. Although the president's selection of a cabinet had been based on political considerations rather than talent, Polk relied heavily on the collective and individual wisdom of its six members. Virtually every major decision at the executive level during the next four years would be made in these meetings. The president invited and encouraged his advisers to express their views on matters that did not pertain to their departmental responsibilities, generally refraining from making his own views known until every department head had spoken. It was not unknown for him to yield if the opinion of the majority was against him, although Polk did not hesitate to disregard their advice if he felt certain he was right. More often than not, however, the group of six like-minded Democrats managed, with the president's prodding, to reach a consensus.

A stern and exacting taskmaster, Polk expected those around him to share his unceasing attention to public affairs. In a fit of pique after his nephew Walker had taken an unscheduled holiday, the president observed, "In truth he is too fond of spending his time in fashionable & light society, and does not give that close & systematic attention to business which is necessary. This I have observed for some months with great regret." Cabinet members were reprimanded for similar lassitude. Whereas it had been customary in past administrations for the executive branch to curtail its operations when Congress was not in session, Polk informed his department heads that their presence would be required in Washington on a full-time basis.

Armed with a prodigious memory and a punctilious sense of detail, the president prided himself on his masterful grasp of the inner workings of the federal bureaucracy. He insisted on regular reports from each cabinet member on departmental affairs, and often dealt directly with their bureau chiefs. "I prefer to supervise the whole operations of the Government myself rather than entrust the public business to subordinates," he wrote.

Frugal by nature and philosophically opposed to big government, Polk kept an especially close eye on federal purse strings. The president urged his cabinet members to be vigilant to waste and mismanagement, and dealt swiftly with public servants accused of criminal misconduct. On learning that a federal land agent in Ohio was in arrears to the amount of $7,100, Polk had him removed from office, filled the vacant post, and initiated criminal proceedings against the defaulter in less than three hours. To set the standard for republican virtue he expected of all federal jobholders, the president shunned ostentatious display at the White House. When Congress allocated funds for the refurbishment of the executive mansion, Polk announced he would spend only half the amount. Scrupulously avoiding any hint of impropriety, the president made it a policy to receive gifts of only modest value. A book or a cane was acceptable, but expensive gifts, such as a fine race horse presented to him by one admirer, and a carriage offered by the citizens of New York, were politely returned.

Supervising the day-to-day operations of the federal government represented only part of the president's official duties. Polk resented the ceremonial functions of his office, which kept him from more pressing matters. Particularly galling were the frequent visits of European diplomats, who arrived at the White House to formally notify the president of the impending marriages, births, and deaths of royal family members. Polk regarded the protocol of European courts with a mixture of bewilderment and disdain. "Such ceremonies," he remarked, "seem very ridiculous to an American."

True to his Jacksonian convictions, Polk adopted none of the trappings of an "imperial presidency." The executive mansion, commonly known in Polk's day as the President's House, was a constant hub of activity for the citizens of Washington, a symbol of a sovereign people that served the function of community center as well as private residence. On Wednesday afternoons, the Marine Corps band played on the White House lawn. Two evenings a week the first family hosted receptions open to the general public, in which members of Congress and the diplomatic corps rubbed shoulders with private citizens.

Sarah Polk was by all accounts much more comfortable in such settings than her socially maladroit husband, and the president relied heavily on her grace and charm to make these events a success. Equally at ease with foreign dignitaries, politicians, and the general public, Sarah won high praise from Washington society, despite her decision to prohibit dancing at the White House, a form of entertainment she found "indecorous." In contrast to her partisan

Polk and members of his cabinet. Seated, from left: John Y. Mason, Attorney General; William H. Marcy, Secretary of War; James K. Polk; Robert J. Walker, Secretary of the Treasury. Standing, from left: Cave Johnson, Postmaster General; George Bancroft, Secretary of the Navy. Missing is Polk's Secretary of State, James Buchanan. Courtesy of the James K. Polk Memorial Assn., Columbia, TN.

husband, she remained on cordial terms with some of the president's fiercest political rivals, among them Henry Clay. Even Boston abolitionist Charles Sumner, who found little to admire in the policies of the chief executive from Tennessee, confessed after a visit to the White House that the first lady's "sweetness of manner, won me entirely."

Four mornings per week, the first servant of the American people made himself available to the general public. Throngs of visitors milled about the downstairs rooms as they waited for an audience with the president, while some felt at liberty to wander about the executive mansion. Johanna Rucker, one of Sarah Polk's nieces who resided at the White House for two years, complained "There is but little privacy here." The executive mansion "belongs to the Government and everyone feels at home and they sometimes stalk into our bedroom and say they are looking at the house."

Among the president's frequent visitors, often as many as a half-dozen each day, were citizens asking for money. Some came to solicit charitable donations for churches, schools, or similar institutions, while others appealed frankly to the president on their own behalf. "The idea seems to prevail with many persons that the President is from his position compelled to contribute to every loafer who applies," the exasperated Polk confided to his diary. As a rule the president denied such requests, "except in a few cases where I am satisfied that the persons applying are objects of charity or in great distress."

Toward the end of his term of office, an elderly, respectably dressed woman from Alexandria, Virginia, visited the president with a request for financial assistance. Polk suggested she seek help from her family and friends, at which the woman became more insistent, naming a specific sum that she had in mind. "I declined to give it to her and was compelled at last to tell her plainly that I did not know her or that she was worthy." When Polk asked again why she did not look to her friends for assistance, the woman replied, much to his surprise, that she did not want them to know of her needy condition. Better to ask the president of the United States for money, she had decided, than to suffer such an indignity.

Polk was more generous in the case of Felix McConnell, an Alabama congressman and long-time friend of the president. When McConnell, an unstable alcoholic, asked to borrow $100, Polk "had not the moral courage to refuse." He would soon have cause to regret this act of charity. Two days later McConnell committed suicide, but not before making it widely known that he had received a substantial sum of money from the president of the United States. "My kindness to poor McConnell," Polk wrote in his diary a few days later, has "brought upon me a horde of beggars who seem to think it is a fine opportunity to supply their wants."

Even more odious to Polk were the hordes of office-seekers who daily encamped at the White House, begging the president to appoint them to federal positions. In the early days of his presidency, Polk dealt with this problem with his customary stoicism. "It is a great and useless consumption of my time, and yet I do not see how I am to avoid it without being rude or insulting, which it is not in my nature to be," he grumbled. During the course of the next four years, Polk's patience would wear exceedingly thin, and by the end of his term he came to regard as "the very scum of society" the patronage-seekers who pestered him for federal jobs.

Polk was not opposed to patronage in principle; as a congressman, he had on occasion recommended persons for federal office if he could vouch for their integrity, and as president he would appoint his brother William to the post of chargé d'affaires to Naples. But Polk utterly deplored the practice by which elected officials used patronage to curry favor with constituents, often petitioning him to appoint individuals they did not know, or in some cases with the knowledge that the applicants were undeserving or unfit for the position.

So great was the demand for political spoils among Democratic partisans that it was a rare day indeed when no visitors requesting federal jobs appeared in Polk's office. One individual asked to be appointed a minister abroad because "he thought he would be a good hand at making treaties," a petition Polk found to be no more unreasonable than most. The sons of prominent Democrats could be particularly obnoxious if the president did not grant them preferential treatment. Such was the case when Lewis Cass Jr., the son of the Michigan senator, asked to be appointed chargé d'affaires to Rome. When the president demurred, Cass "manifested great anxiety and was scarcely rational on the subject." Polk ultimately relented and gave the young man the post he desired. But for every vacancy filled, there were several disappointed office-seekers. Thomas Hart Benton's son John was reportedly drunk when he arrived at the White House to demand a lieutenant's commission in the army. Polk pointed out that there were others more worthy of consideration, prompting Benton to fly into a rage, leaving the president's office "very rudely, swearing profusely as he went out of the door."

Little wonder, then, that the president described his job as "no bed of roses." In his diary, Polk complained frequently of the burdens of his office and longed for the day when he could return to private life. In view of his taxing schedule, the president could hardly be accused of exaggeration when he declared, "I am the hardest working man in this country."

Still, the frequency with which he felt the need to remind himself of his herculean labors is revealing. The president viewed himself as a simple public servant, toiling without respite on behalf of the nation. He had nothing but self-righteous contempt, on the other hand, for others who made politics their profession, regarding them as party hacks and office-seekers. Their unbridled pursuit of their own interests made him "almost ready at times to conclude that all men are selfish, and that there is no reliance to be placed in any of the human race." No doubt Polk derived considerable gratification from the status, power, and honor that were the rewards of high office, but he could not admit to himself that he coveted these things. When the chief executive traveled beyond the capital, he explicitly ordered that no pomp or ceremony should attend the presidential entourage; privately, however, he was not displeased when these instructions were ignored. Polk viewed his one-term pledge in much the same way: as irrefutable evidence that he did not desire political power for its own sake. Although his offer to serve only one term had initially been made in the interests of party unity, in time it became for Polk the ultimate test of self-abnegation. When urged to reconsider his decision he remained unmoved, insisting that he had no greater wish than to return to private life after fulfilling his duty to the nation.

The next session of Congress did not convene until the end of the year, giving the new president nine months to establish his control over the executive branch and the Washington bureaucracy. True to his desire to "be *myself* President of the U.S.," Polk undertook a thorough purge of federal office-holders, sweeping out scores of government workers who owed their jobs to the previous Whig administration. Democrats of suspect loyalties were also eliminated. Polk unceremoniously dumped long-time Jackson ally Francis Blair, who had served for 14 years as the publisher of the Democratic party's official newspaper in Washington. Determined to have a man of his own choosing as the party's editorial spokesman, a role that he viewed as no less important than a cabinet post, Polk ordered Blair to sell his newspaper to a group of investors, which then installed Virginia newspaperman Thomas Ritchie as editor and renamed the publication the Washington *Union*.

When the Twenty-ninth Congress convened in December 1845, it found the administration ready to do battle on behalf of its legislative agenda. The new president had little faith in the ability of so fractious a body as the U.S. Congress to shape public policy; rather, he believed that it was the function of the executive branch to initiate legislation and work aggressively to build a consensus for its programs on Capitol Hill. For Polk, "the most important domestic measure of my administration" was the passage of a lower tariff. As a candidate in the 1844 campaign, Polk had played skillfully on the public's dissatisfaction with the protective tariff enacted by the Whigs in 1842. Though willing to support a tariff high enough to raise revenue to pay for the operating expenses of the federal government, Polk had opposed protectionism throughout his career. Increasingly apprehensive of industrial and urban growth, the president believed that high tariffs served only to enrich business interests at the expense of the laboring classes. A free trade policy, on the other hand, would help to forestall these dangerous trends, offering increased export opportunities for American farmers, and in so doing would help to preserve the agrarian economic order.

Polk's nostalgic vision of a pastoral America was not universally shared by the leaders of his party. In northern states, some Democratic congressmen balked at incurring the wrath of manufacturing constituencies, which were determined to resist any tampering with the Whig tariff of 1842. This was particularly true in Pennsylvania, where powerful coal and iron interests could not easily be ignored, even by the most stalwart Democrats. The administration's tariff position was a sensitive subject for Secretary of State Buchanan and Vice-President Dallas, both of whom feared their leadership within the Keystone state Democracy would be ruined by their association with a lower tariff.

Congress took its time responding to the president's call for tariff reform, which was both a complex and controversial undertaking. The bill involved revising the schedule of duties on hundreds of separate articles, many of which encountered stiff resistance from American producers anxious to protect their markets from foreign competition.

Foreign policy crises with Great Britain and Mexico (to be discussed in subsequent chapters) also diverted the attention of Congress from domestic legislation. Thus it was not until mid-April 1846 that a tariff bill which had been carefully drafted by Secretary of the Treasury Robert J. Walker emerged from the House Ways and Means Committee. Further delays would occur before the bill came to a vote, allowing opponents more time to lobby against the new rate schedule. Critics charged that the tariff would let loose a flood of British-made goods on the American market, destroying domestic manufacturing and, in the process, the very economic freedoms they had fought two wars against Great Britain to protect. Cried one Whig congressman from Vermont: "Are all the exertions and sufferings of our fathers in the Revolution, to redeem us from this state of colonial dependence, to be, in effect, set aside and disregarded, and our much-boasted independence be bartered away for *cheap clothing and necessaries,* which we are fully able ourselves to provide?" In a last-ditch attempt to exert pressure on the nation's lawmakers, manufacturers held an elaborate trade fair in Washington to display their goods. The president visited the exposition, but came away more convinced than ever that American manufacturers "should rely upon their own resources," and "not upon the bounty of the Government . . . for their support."

After countless modifications to the bill in an effort to satisfy wavering Democrats, administration forces in the House finally felt confident enough to allow the measure to come up for a vote. Even so, 18 northern Democrats, including all but one of the 12 Democrats from Pennsylvania, remained unmoved by administration pressure and voted against the bill. Despite their opposition, the measure passed by a comfortable 19-vote margin on July 3, 1846.

In the Senate, where the Democrats clung to a bare three-vote majority, even stiffer resistance could be expected.

For two hot weeks in July, the fate of the tariff reform bill hung in the balance. There were rumors of bribed votes; Polk was shocked to learn, rather naively perhaps, that one Democratic senator had been offered a personal loan by a wealthy businessman in exchange for a vote against the bill. One senator from North Carolina resigned rather than obey his state legislature, which had instructed him to vote for the measure. Another lawmaker, hoping to avoid taking a stand on the tariff issue altogether, found pressing business in his home state that required his immediate attention and prepared to leave town. Friends of the president caught up with the senator at the train station and prevailed on him to return to the White House. After Polk made a final, hour-long appeal, the senator agreed to remain in Washington and vote for the bill. Vice-President Dallas, whose vote as president of the Senate would be required in the event of a tie, also agonized over his decision. After much soul searching he resolved to support the administration bill, despite the measure's enormous unpopularity in his home state. In the end his vote was not needed, the Senate passing the so-called Walker Tariff by a one-vote margin.

A far less controversial part of the administration's domestic agenda was the Independent Treasury bill, which the president hoped would be the final word in the long debate over the federal government's proper relationship with the banking system. When Andrew Jackson removed federal deposits from the Bank of the United States with Polk's assistance in the 1830s, they had been placed in private, state-chartered institutions, known by Jackson's enemies as "pet banks." Such a policy did not go far enough to satisfy hard-money Democrats, who were suspicious of all banks, and who argued that in crushing one "monster" they had only created several smaller ones. Martin Van Buren had managed near the end of his term to win passage of a bill establishing an Independent Treasury system, which removed federal funds from circulation entirely, placing them in government vaults until such time as they were needed to meet federal expenses. The Tyler administration had scrapped the plan, however, returning federal deposits to regional banks.

The Independent Treasury bill caused genuine alarm in the New York business community. Wall Street feared that the removal of federal monies from local banks would result in a shortage of available capital, thereby causing a credit squeeze and financial instability. Unlike the tariff issue, however, Democratic party ranks snapped smartly back into line when the bill came up for a House vote in April. The Whigs put up a desultory resistance to the measure, but in the absence of defections from the other side of the aisle, there was little they could do. The Senate approved the bill in June, with the balloting once again following straight party lines.

While Congress bowed to the executive yoke on tariff and fiscal policy, it proved to be more intractable on the issue of internal improvements. Like his Democratic predecessors, Polk took the view that transportation projects were a state and local concern. But in recent years these sentiments were in conspicuous retreat among many Democrats. As American farmers pushed farther westward, away from the eastern urban centers which served as markets for their produce, they required sophisticated, interstate transportation networks that only the national government could provide. The cry for federally funded internal improvements was loudest in the new western states, whose governments lacked sufficient capital resources to finance such schemes. Even in the South, where the philosophy of limited government permeated the fabric of its political culture, support for internal improvements was gaining ground. In 1845, western and southern business and political leaders had gathered at a meeting in Memphis to discuss the feasibility of a project to develop the Mississippi River, chaired by none other than states' rights champion John C. Calhoun.

The president was forced to address the issue of internal improvements when Congress passed a rivers and harbors bill in the summer of 1846. Polk was so strongly opposed to the idea that he departed from his normal practice of soliciting the advice of his cabinet. Suspecting that several members approved of the measure, the president merely informed them of his decision to veto the bill. Polk took the opportunity in his veto message to state his strict constructionist views, arguing that the Constitution gave the federal government no clear authority to fund a system of internal improvements. In addition to his constitutional objections, the president maintained that such a program would also produce sectional prejudices, since federal largesse could not be distributed equally to all the states. It would, morever, be unfair to those states that had already taken the lead in building their own transportation systems with local funds. And once a precedent for federal involvement had been established, Polk feared, the government would be required to fund all projects, regardless of merit, thus igniting "a disreputable scramble for the public money" by state and local authorities and their representatives in Washington.

A House vote to override the presidential veto fell well short of the required two-thirds majority, and with only a few days of the congressional session remaining, the internal improvements bill was dead for the present. Congress returned to the issue when it reconvened in December, but once again a bill did not emerge from the legislature until the end of the session, allowing the president to defeat the measure with a pocket veto. Determined to put an end to congressional interest in internal improvements once and for all, Polk restated his views at length in his fourth annual message. For Polk, the issue of internal improvements could not be uncoupled from the long train of anti-Jacksonian economic policies that he had opposed for almost a quarter of a century in public life. Should the nation's leaders sanction a program of public works projects, he believed, "it will necessarily and speedily draw after it the reestablishment of a national bank, the revival of a protective tariff" and other Whig measures. No less vigilant to threats from the "money power" than he had been when he served as a Jackson lieutenant in the bank war, Polk stood ready to block any proposal that in his mind would give "the favored classes undue control and sway in our Government." Congress would continue to debate a number of internal improvements bills during the remaining months of the president's term, but none would pass, eliminating the need for further executive action.

The Whigs excoriated the president for his economic policies, predicting imminent disaster for farmer and manufacturer alike. But the calamities the opposition feared never materialized. In part, this was due to the fact that the new tariff bill had not completely abandoned American manufacturers to foreign competition, as the Whigs claimed. While iron duties dropped significantly, from 40 percent to 30 percent, the Walker tariff was not low enough to inundate the American market with less expensive European-made products. In fact, these losses were more than offset by a dramatic rise in the export of heavy industrial goods, fueled by a railroad-building boom in Europe. American farmers fared even better than manufacturers during the Polk years. In addition to the administration's free trade policy, which as expected opened up new markets for American farm goods, agricultural producers benefited from crop failures in Europe. In the wake of the Irish potato famine, wheat exports rose a remarkable 300 percent in a single year.

Despite the administration's legislative successes, several indicators pointed to a president increasingly out of step with important segments of his party on economic matters. To many Democrats, Polk's rigid adherence to laissez-faire principles seemed ill-suited to meet the challenges of a sophisticated marketplace. In the North, party stalwarts chafed at his obdurate refusal to placate powerful business constituencies; in the West, Democrats were irritated by the parsimonious president's manifest reluctance to subsidize the nation's transportation infrastructure. In growing numbers, Democrats were joining Whig nationalists in calling for a greater federal role in promoting economic development.

Such dissatisfaction within the ranks showed few signs of flaring into open rebellion, however. Democrats could hardly express their unhappiness too loudly; Polk's policies, after all, had long been regarded as litmus tests of party membership, the Democratic coalition having already weathered divisive struggles over such economic issues as the tariff and the bank in Jackson's day. Instead, a new set of challenges, far more threatening to party unity than those the Democrats had faced in the past, was already taking shape. This time, the battle for the soul of the party would be waged in the arena of foreign affairs.

6

The Course of Empire

In 1845, the United States exuded the self-confidence of a world power. Since the founding of the republic a little more than half a century earlier, the nation had experienced a sevenfold increase in population. The national domain had more than doubled; the original 13 states now numbered 27, with another, Texas, waiting to be admitted into the Union. The Panic of 1837 had given way to a new climate of prosperity. By any standard, the United States was a young nation on the rise.

Evidence of growth and material progress was only partly responsible for the prevailing mood of national self-congratulation. Americans derived enormous satisfaction from their belief that other peoples throughout the world were following their example in setting up republican institutions. The American political experiment, they noted proudly, had emboldened revolutionaries in Europe and South America, toppling governments and undermining monarchical rule. In Great Britain, the working-class Chartist movement threatened to break the power of the aristocracy, calling for universal male suffrage and a new egalitarian social order. Americans immodestly claimed credit for these developments, convinced that their political system represented the vanguard of civilization. The New York *Herald* editorialized in 1845: "A spirit has taken wing from the land of freedom which is destined to carry civil and religious liberty to the ends of the earth." Even the most meditative of American writers indulged in the exuberant jingoism of the age. "America," Ralph Waldo Emerson declared, "is the country of the Future."

National chauvinism was not unique to the United States, but was part of a much broader cultural phenomenon evident in Europe and throughout the western hemisphere. Latin American intellectuals, whose countries had recently won their independence from Spain and Portugal, often exhibited a patriotism equal in ardor to their northern neighbors, while in Europe the collapse of the Napoleonic Empire had prompted nationalist strivings that could be seen from the Iberian peninsula to the Balkans. American notions of cultural uniqueness were borrowed in large part from the Romantic movement then flourishing in western Europe, which held that special, innate characteristics stamped each people with an identity of its own. Nonetheless, such ideas struck a particularly responsive chord among Americans, who had long sensed they were marked for greatness.

If nationalism in all its various manifestations was everywhere on the rise, nowhere did it permeate so fully the collective mindset of a people than in the United States. Popular nationalism had emerged largely as a consequence of the new democratic culture; the right to vote had given white American males a vested interest in their national government, which translated not only into active participation in the pageantry of politics, but in a deep-seated pride in all things American. French observer Alexis de Tocqueville noted: "As the American participates in all that is done in his country, he thinks himself obliged to defend whatever may be censured in it; for it is not only his country that is attacked, it is himself."

It was no small irony that rampant nationalism could thrive at a time when sectional problems over such issues as the tariff and slavery were becoming increasingly vexatious. But Americans did not allow regional rivalries and antagonisms to stand in the way of their reverence for national institutions. English visitor Frances Trollope found no lack of sectional prejudices, but everywhere heard the sentiment that "the American government was the best in the world." Foreign visitors almost without exception commented, often disapprovingly, on the inordinate pride Americans took in their accomplishments as a people. Boston Unitarian minister William E. Channing agreed, observing of his countrymen: "An American has a passion for belonging to a great country."

By the 1840s, territorial expansion was viewed by many to be a measure of that greatness. The westward surge of the early nineteenth century had fired the American imagination. With Texas on the verge of admission into the Union, Americans began to direct their gaze toward new, unsettled western lands. At the time of Polk's inaugural, a new generation of pioneers was wending its way through the Rocky Mountains en route to settlements in Oregon's Willamette Valley. Nothing, it seemed, could stop or even slow the Anglo-American advance.

As a result, citizens of the United States were drawn irresistibly to the conclusion that theirs was a nation ordained by God to establish a continental empire that would be the envy of the world. In 1845, John L. O'Sullivan, a 32-year-old newspaper editor, gave the country a catchphrase that seemed to define the expansive mood. America had a "manifest destiny," O'Sullivan wrote, "to overspread the continent allotted by Providence for the free development of our yearly multiplying millions."

The potency of the term Manifest Destiny lay in its ambiguity, for expansionism was a program of many agendas. For all their new-found nationalism, Americans still retained their parochial focus, viewing Manifest Destiny in terms of the benefits that would accrue to their own particular region. Not all parts of the country shared the same expansionist objectives. Southern "cotton" Democrats regarded the annexation of Texas as a holy crusade, while in the West the burning issue for many was the question of American title to the Oregon territory. Although some ultraexpansionists managed to rise above their loyalty to section, and in their most fanciful moments could see no limit to American dominion, they constituted only a small part of the Manifest Destiny phenomenon.

Similarly, a variety of opinions existed regarding the methods by which these goals would be fulfilled. O'Sullivan himself was uncertain about what steps the United States should take to realize its territorial ambitions and changed his mind more than once on the subject. Some militant advocates of Manifest Destiny favored rapid expansion and the bold pursuit of American claims to Texas and Oregon, even at the risk of war with Mexico and Great Britain. Others, no less committed to the long-term goal of an American empire, opposed the use of force to achieve these ends, believing that contiguous lands would voluntarily join the Union in order to obtain the blessings and benefits of republican rule. In an often-used metaphor of the day, these regions would ripen like fruit and fall into the lap of the United States. The imminent annexation of Texas was merely the first step in a process by which the country would acquire a transcontinental empire. This imperial destiny would be achieved by peaceful means, a testament to the superiority of Anglo-American institutions. There were, then, many advocates of Manifest Destiny, who viewed the concept in different ways. All, however, were bound by the belief that American expansion was inspired and ordained by a Divine Providence.

Despite their long tradition of westward movement, Americans had not always thought of their nation in continental terms. In the late eighteenth century, the United States seemed to have land enough; even before the Louisiana Purchase Thomas Jefferson could confidently declare that the national domain would satisfy the needs of American farmers for the "thousandth and thousandth" generation. The Far West held little attraction for many Americans, whose knowledge of the region was sketchy and often incorrect. The government-sponsored expeditions of Zebulon Pike in 1806 and Stephen Long in 1820 had done little to spark the nation's interest in the vast wilderness that lay beyond its existing borders. Describing the area as unsuitable for agricultural development, their discouraging reports did much to popularize the myth of the West as a "Great American Desert."

Philosophically, the Jeffersonians had long harbored serious misgivings about westward expansion. Since the founding of the Republic, many Americans had worried that large nations were incompatible with popular sovereignty. The French political theorist Montesquieu had warned that empires could be governed only by a strong central power, a system that would inevitably lead to tyranny. James Madison felt compelled to refute this theory in *The Federalist,* arguing that a federal republic, in which the people delegated their political duties to elected representatives, would function as effectively as a pure democracy. Far from endangering civil liberties, Madison argued, such a system would actually safeguard them, for the diffusion of power would inhibit the emergence of factions so inimical to a free, virtuous body politic. Even many Jeffersonians, however, were not entirely convinced by this line of reasoning. As late as 1824, President James Monroe found it hard to conceive of a continental destiny for the United States, believing that the territory west of the Rocky Mountains would be peopled by Anglo-American settlers who would establish an independent sister republic of their own.

By the time James K. Polk took the oath of office in 1845, many of these concerns had ceased to exert much influence on American public opinion. The earlier misconceptions about the West had been completely dispelled by a new generation of American explorers and adventurers. Richard Henry Dana's autobiographical novel, *Two Years Before the Mast,* had awakened Americans to the vast, untapped potential of California. Naval officer Charles Wilkes, who undertook a three-year fact-finding voyage of the Pacific, provided much valuable information of the continent's western coastline. Perhaps the most successful promoter of the Far West was John Charles Frémont, whose exploratory missions on behalf of the U.S. Army in 1842 and 1843 excited the imagination of policy makers and public alike. These and a host of lesser-known boosters all helped to focus the nation's attention on the drive westward.

The gradual and successful settlement of the immense Louisiana territory had quieted fears that expansion might endanger republicanism. Indeed, by the 1840s many Democrats had come to believe that expansion held the key to the very survival of Jefferson's agrarian legacy. An abundance of land was viewed as the mainstay of a prosperous republic, providing economic opportunity for millions. Without territorial growth, Polk and others feared, the diffusion of economic and political power would be checked, and the emergence of a monied elite would surely follow. Only expansion could provide the antidote to consolidation. "As our boundaries have been enlarged and our agricultural population has been spread over a large surface, our federative system has acquired additional strength and security," the president stated in his inaugural address. "It is confidently believed that our system may be safely extended to the utmost bounds of our territorial limits, and that as it shall be extended the bonds of our Union, so far from being weakened, will become stronger."

But the nation's resources, unlimited though they may have seemed, were not inexhaustible. Creeping urbanization and a rising tide of immigrants from Germany and Ireland worried many expansionists, who viewed Manifest Destiny as a means to obtain a new lease on the Jeffersonian ideal. Expansionism, then, offered a way of ensuring that future generations would enjoy the blessings afforded by an agrarian society.

A changing political climate was also responsible for the nation's insatiable appetite for new lands. Democratic politicians thought they had found in the issue of expansionism a means to defuse the slavery issue that threatened to divide both the country and the party. The desire for Texas in the slaveholding states could not be ignored, as Martin Van Buren's fate at the Democratic convention in Baltimore had amply demonstrated. By broadening the list of expansionist objectives to include northern and northwestern interests, Democrats hoped to curtail the damage done to party unity.

A new breed of newspaper publishers also lent its growing influence to the expansionist crusade. With the development of the steam printing press in the 1830s and the rotary cylinder press a decade later, publishers were now able to dramatically cut printing costs and increase production, making the rise of the mass circulation newspaper possible. Unlike party-sponsored news organs, the "penny press" relied on circulation and advertising as its principal sources of revenue, and therefore enjoyed the freedom to take independent positions on the major issues of the day. Publishers such as John L. O'Sullivan of the New York *Morning News,* James Gordon Bennett of the New York *Herald,* and Moses Beach of the New York *Sun,* discovered that empire building made good copy and sold newspapers. In an article titled "More! More! More!," the *Morning News* exulted: "the whole boundless continent is ours." In the rush to celebrate the new expansionist spirit, the penny press sought to outdo one another in scaling new heights of hyperbole. "The flight of the eagle is toward the west," crowed the *Herald*, "and there it is he spreads his wings for freedom."

The boundless optimism that fueled this expansive spirit was also the result of a transportation and communications revolution that made the prospect of a continental Union possible. One by one, nature's barriers were surrendering to human ingenuity. Steamboats defied currents and paddled upriver, turning America's waterways into bustling commercial thoroughfares, binding the nation into a cohesive and interdependent economic unit. A network of railroads had integrated eastern markets and was now providing connecting links with towns and cities on the western slope of the Appalachians. "This world is going on too fast," observed Philip Hone, a New York merchant. "Railroads, steamers, packets, race against time and beat it hollow. . . . Oh, for the good old days of heavy post-coaches and speed at the rate of six miles an hour!" Most extraordinary of all was the telegraph, which was first used to carry the news of Polk's nomination from Baltimore to Washington, D.C. During the next four years 10,000 miles of wire would be laid across the country. Hone marveled that the invention had "annihilated all space, and tied the two ends of a continent in a knot!" An American dominion stretching from the Atlantic to the Pacific, once the pipedream of visionaries, now seemed within reach.

Southerners anxious to enlarge the slave empire were among the most vehement champions of expansion. The annexation of Texas would give the United States complete control over all the known cotton-growing lands in

North America, thus ensuring an American monopoly over this vitally important resource. New slave states would not only enhance the South's political power; they would also serve as an outlet for its surplus slaves. While the importation of slaves had officially ended in 1808, the black population of the Deep South was increasing at a faster rate than that of whites. This was an ominous trend for slaveowners, who lived in constant fear of the "peculiar institution" even as they vowed to defend it at all costs. The Denmark Vesey conspiracy in 1822 and Nat Turner rebellion in 1831 had awakened southern whites to their precarious situation. More recently, a plot to incite a slave rebellion in Cuba had been uncovered in 1844, offering another reminder that repressive measures alone could not guarantee the safety of the planter class. Only by extending the boundaries of slavery, then, could southern whites relieve the demographic pressures caused by a growing slave population that might one day rise up and overwhelm them.

Still another element of the expansionist impulse was the lure of foreign markets. For many years, merchant ships laden with tea and silk from China, tallow and hides from California, and furs from Oregon had deposited their cargoes on the wharves of Boston and New York. The need for way stations en route to the Orient had made Hawaii a bustling Yankee outpost long before Caleb Cushing, the U.S. commissioner to China, signed a treaty in 1844 opening five Chinese ports to American commerce. As the United States assumed a prominent role in the global marketplace, politicians of both parties became aware of the desirability of outlets on the Pacific. The strategic and commercial advantages of San Francisco— "one of the finest, if not the very best harbour in the world," according to U.S. navy reports—had aroused considerable interest among Washington policy makers.

The disastrous Panic of 1837, which had resulted in huge surpluses and depressed prices for American farm products, also focused attention on the need for new foreign markets.

Finally, a fear of Great Britain gave American expansionism a special sense of urgency. Americans had long been suspicious of British activities in the western hemisphere, but inevitably this fear had grown as the United States began to define its strategic and economic interests in terms that extended beyond its own borders. Not since the War of 1812 had Americans indulged in such rampant Anglophobia. Democrats denounced the 1842 Webster-Ashburton treaty, which settled a long-simmering dispute over the Canada–Maine boundary, as a betrayal of American interests. A showdown between the United States and Great Britain over Oregon seemed inevitable, given the new administration's bold campaign pledge to disregard British claims to the territory. The close relationship between Great Britain and Mexico, a friendship cemented by sizable loans from British banks, was also a matter of great concern to expansionists. American commercial interests viewed Great Britain as the only power that might prevent the United States from gaining control of Mexico's highly prized ports on the Pacific coast. Everywhere they turned, expansionists saw Great Britain blocking their territorial ambitions. As much as any single factor, it was this fear of British encirclement that converted many supporters of gradual expansion into apostles of the new imperialism.

Among southern slaveowners, fear of British machinations in North America had reached almost hysterical proportions. Great Britain had abolished slavery in its colonial possessions in 1833, a move that sent shock waves through the South's slaveholding community. By the 1840s, John C. Calhoun and other southern statesmen alleged, on the basis of little evidence, that Great Britain was actively engaged in a plot to promote abolitionism throughout North America. Reports that British diplomats were seeking to use their influence with Mexico to persuade that government to recognize Texas as a sovereign nation gave rise to wild speculation in the South regarding British intentions. One rumor alleged that Her Majesty's government had demanded the emancipation of Texas slaves as the price of its intercession on the Republic's behalf (such a plan had been suggested by at least one hopeful British diplomat, but the scheme had fallen on deaf ears in Whitehall). As a haven for free black labor and runaway slaves on the southwestern border of the United States, an independent Texas Republic would undermine the institution in the Deep South. Some southerners believed that British activities in Texas represented an even more immediate and direct threat to their security. According to one grim scenario, Great Britain planned to launch a full-scale invasion of the United States, using Texas as a staging area, where it would be poised to strike at New Orleans, the gateway to the Mississippi River valley.

The Anglophobia that gripped the United States in the 1840s was not simply a response to British activities, real or imagined, in the western hemisphere. If American political leaders and the general public were inclined to exaggerate that fear, it was due in large part to the fact that hostility toward the British had long been a vital part of American political culture. Since its inception, the young nation defined itself in the context of its revolutionary struggle against Great Britain. Although 30 years had passed since Andrew Jackson's victory at New Orleans, Anglophobia showed no signs of abating; for politicians like James K. Polk, Robert J. Walker, and James Buchanan, who represented a new generation of Democratic statesmen too young to participate in the country's two wars for independence, hostility toward Great Britain was an article of faith, a means of affirming their commitment to the revolutionary tradition of their forefathers. This was particularly true of Polk, who had been greatly embarrassed by allegations that his grandfather harbored Loyalist sympathies during the Revolutionary War. The strident republicanism of the nation's new leaders was a self-conscious repudiation of the Old World values they associated with Great Britain. Political independence had been won; the country now sought to sever the cultural ties that were the last remaining vestiges of its colonial past. The Jacksonian assault against aristocracy and privilege, culminating in the killing of the Bank of the United States, had been a conspicuous part of this ongoing effort to establish a new social order based on republican principles. But such ideological ardor was not self-sustaining; new enemies of liberty had to be uncovered to keep the revolutionary flame alive.

No American public figure was more alarmed by the British menace than Andrew Jackson. In near-apocalyptic terms the aging dragon-slayer warned that if Great Britain managed to establish a permanent foothold on the continent it "would cost oceans of blood and millions of money to Burst asunder." From the Hermitage, he scrawled anxious messages to his protegé in the White House, warning him to stand firm against the British in Oregon and Texas. "War is a blessing," Jackson wrote to the president-elect shortly before his death, "compared with national degradation." As they had done before in their battle against the "Monster Bank," the Jacksonians heeded their leader's call to arms and girded themselves for combat against the foes of republican virtue.

Thus by the mid–1840s continentalism was ready to assume center stage. The new expansionists were a motley collection of interest groups, motivated by a welter of widely divergent issues, and articulating a broad range of uniquely American hopes and fears. If the agenda for empire remained unclear, one thing, at least, was certain: the nation's fitful, desultory efforts to expand its domain would now give way to a deliberate, aggressive, and impatient policy to extend American hegemony across the continent.

Ironically, this outpouring of national chauvinism raised disturbing questions about the kind of nation the United States had become. Americans had long believed that their nation had been chosen by Providence to serve as a beacon of liberty, guiding the Old World out of the darkness of monarchical despotism. This special sense of mission, however, seemed jarringly inconsistent with the strident, often bellicose demand for more land. Could the United States, in its new incarnation as an imperial power, remain true to the ideals on which it had been founded? Could it continue to present itself as a moral exemplar for other nations, even as it boldly asserted its right to establish a continental empire?

Yes, insisted the advocates of Manifest Destiny, who developed a formidable array of arguments to justify their imperial agenda. Chief among them was the contention that territorial expansion represented a new phase of the republican experiment; far from being inconsistent with the ideology of liberty, the acquisition of new lands would widen the sphere in which republicanism could operate. Secretary of State James Buchanan believed that the American people had "a great and glorious mission to perform . . . extending the blessings of Christianity and of civil and religious liberty over the whole of the North American continent." The *Democratic Review,* a journal published by John L. O'Sullivan, echoed these sentiments. "We are the nation of human progress," O'Sullivan proclaimed, "and who will, what can, set limits to our onward march?"

Such lofty rhetoric obscured the fact that the idealism which had inspired earlier generations of Americans was now in full retreat. Even as they called on other nations to follow their lead and establish republican institutions, Americans were beginning to suspect that they alone possessed the requisite qualities for self-government. The great task of planting these institutions beyond the boundaries of the United States could not be entrusted to the nonwhite peoples with whom they shared the continent. The seedlings of democracy would instead be carried by waves of American migrants, to germinate and flower in foreign soils. Americans continued to trumpet their commitment to liberty, but rather than lead by example they now claimed the right to "extend the area of freedom" by enlarging their own domain. The mission to uplift and regenerate humankind had become little more than a clever rationale for national aggrandizement.

As Manifest Destiny gained momentum, expansionist politicians and pundits cast off all pretense of altruism, boldly asserting their claim to the continent on the grounds that the land belonged to those best able to develop it. All legal rights of ownership were nullified by an obligation to a higher authority—Divine Providence—to make the land fruitful and productive. White Americans had repeatedly invoked the argument of territorial utility to defend the expropriation of Indian lands in the years following the War of 1812. The same rationale could also be employed with good effect to justify U.S. claims in the Pacific Northwest. Unlike American settlers in Oregon's Willamette Valley, the British had no interest in the region's agricultural potential, confining their commercial operations to trapping the fur-bearing animals along the Columbia and Snake rivers. Similarly, American expansionists viewed Mexico's tenuous control of its northernmost provinces as an open invitation for conquest. This line of reasoning led one journalist in 1846 to declare that California "belonged not to indolent Mexico but to the people who would use it to scatter God's blessings to mankind."

Increasingly, as Anglo-Americans looked enviously on the vast reaches of the continent they did not possess, they felt compelled to denigrate the people who lived there. Indians and Mexicans came to be seen as obstacles in the path of progress, who would have to be swept aside to allow the great work of civilization to continue. But in order to justify a program of subjugation, the expansionists would first have to establish the inability of non-whites to develop beyond their present condition. While Americans had never accepted the concept of racial equality, during the eighteenth century Enlightenment ideals, which were firmly rooted in a basic faith in human progress, had at least served to temper American racist attitudes. During the first half of the nineteenth century, however, the view that all peoples were capable of improvement gave way to a new and virulent strain of racial prejudice.

The Anglo-American view of Mexico and its seven million inhabitants reflected these changing attitudes. The historic rivalry of Protestant England and Catholic Spain had established a firm foundation of mutual suspicion and distrust. Prospects for a new era of hemispheric harmony brightened when Mexico won its independence in 1821, and three years later adopted a constitution modeled after that of the United States. Flattered by what they perceived to be an attempt to imitate their political system, Americans cheered the creation of a sister republic on their southwestern border. But as Mexican-held Texas became an object of desire for American expansionists, the image of the Mexican in the public mind was transformed from freedom-loving republican to loathesome "greaser." In sharp contrast to their self-image as an industrious and hardy race, Anglo-Americans regarded their Hispanic neighbors as intellectually inferior and morally degenerate, an indolent people who stirred themselves only to satisfy their basic wants and basest passions. The political turmoil that gripped

Mexico following independence was but one consequence of this inferiority, Americans believed, demonstrating that its population was incapable of self-government.

At the same time that racial attitudes were acquiring a new virulence, a host of "scientific" arguments arose to validate them. Apostles of the new expansionism drew freely from the writings of ethnologists who attributed distinguishing racial characteristics to climate and environment. The inhabitants of tropical zones, they argued, were by nature listless and phlegmatic, while those occupying colder regions displayed greater energy and vigor. "All history teaches that the general course of conquest has been from north to south," one Texas writer observed, noting that "animals are more daring and ferocious" in high latitudes, while the hotter climate close to the equator "enervates the system and debases the mind." Such views enjoyed virtually universal acceptance in the United States, even among those who did not share the expansionists' appetite for new lands. Miscegenation—the mixing of races—was another popular argument used to explain what Americans perceived as the cultural backwardness of other peoples. Oblivious to the increasing ethnic heterogeneity of their own society, Americans deplored the racial admixture of Latin America. The *mestizo* population of Mexico represented an altogether inferior hybrid, "a mongrel breed of negroes, Indians, and Spaniards of the baser sort." The new racial theories did not represent a coherent doctrine or school of thought, but were a curious amalgam of science, fad, and wishful thinking. They nonetheless exerted a powerful influence on Americans anxiously looking for rationales for conquest.

Increased contact between the two cultures served only to aggravate Anglo-American racial prejudices. During the 1820s and 1830s thousands of Anglo settlers flocked to Texas, where large parcels of fertile land could be purchased at nominal prices. Although technically citizens of Mexico, most of the new migrants had little regard for Mexican laws or customs. Forming their own ethnic enclaves, they held themselves apart from the *tejano* community and consequently saw no reason to reject the standard view of Mexicans as a shiftless and idle race. Even Stephen F. Austin, who established the first colony of Anglo-Americans in Texas, and who enjoyed for many years a close relationship with Mexican officials, held the general populace in contempt, writing during a trip to Mexico City in 1823 that the denizens of the capital "want nothing but tails to be more brutes than the Apes."

The hostility that characterized relations between Mexicans and Anglo-Americans was fanned to a white heat in 1836 with the Texas Revolution. Three episodes in particular—the slaughter of the Alamo defenders, the execution of Texas prisoners at Goliad, and the utter rout of Mexico's army at San Jacinto—served to sharpen the image of the Mexican in the American mind. Each offered a new dimension to an already unsavory character portrait, enabling Anglos to add cruelty, treachery, and cowardice to the compendium of vices they ascribed to their Latin American neighbors. Racial antagonisms continued to smolder in the decade that followed, and were periodically inflamed by border clashes between Texas and Mexico, producing new stories of alleged Mexican atrocities, all of which were chronicled with grisly relish by the American press.

Secure in their conviction that non-whites were racially inferior, incapable of self-government, or of utilizing fully the natural resources at their disposal, Anglo-Americans could apply themselves to the task of empire building. But if the United States was destined to occupy the continent, what was to become of the non-white peoples that presently inhabited these lands? Once again, the ideology of expansionism had a ready answer: they would recede before the steady march of white civilization; they would simply disappear. The decimation of the North American Indian tribes during the early years of European contact was offered as evidence to support this scenario. In July 1845, the New York *Herald* proclaimed that "all other races . . . must bow and fade" before "the great work of subjugation and conquest to be achieved by the Anglo-Saxon race." Anglo-Americans were quick to suspend logic and accept this extraordinary line of reasoning because it salved the national conscience. To argue that the eradication of entire races was an inevitable process was to exculpate the Anglo-American people; there was, after all, nothing they could do about it.

James K. Polk was in many ways a fitting representative of this expansionist impulse. While the new president did not defend his administration's territorial goals on racial grounds, he never questioned the superiority of Anglo-American institutions, nor harbored the slightest doubt that these institutions were destined to spread inexorably across the continent. In 1845, for both President Polk and the public at large, Manifest Destiny remained inchoate, undefined, an effusive, bumptious spirit rather than a clearly articulated agenda for empire. Although the recent election could not be construed as a mandate for a policy of territorial acquisition—so diverse were the constituencies that subscribed to at least some facet of expansionism—Polk owed his sudden and unexpected return to national prominence to those who dreamed of a larger continental role for the United States. Advocates of the new imperialism now looked to Polk to enlarge the national domain. Most would not be disappointed. The new president immediately placed himself at the head of the expansionist crusade; henceforth he would chart its course and set its objectives. With characteristic resolve, the goal-oriented and methodical chief executive strove to make the rhetoric of Manifest Destiny a reality.

7

All of Texas and All of Oregon

Since the turn of the century, Texas had been a perpetual source of friction between the United States and its Latin American neighbor—a vast wilderness claimed by Spain but coveted by Anglo-Americans as they pushed across the continent. So attractive was the area to expansion-minded Americans that the United States maintained that it had acquired the territory in 1803 as part of the Louisiana Purchase. Although it made little effort to enforce this far-fetched claim, this did not stop American adventurers from periodically leading their own, privately financed "filibuster" expeditions into Texas with the goal of wresting the region away from Spanish control. By the time Washington officially renounced its claim to the land beyond the Sabine River with the Adams-Onís treaty in 1819, southerners had come to view Texas as the next frontier for the expansion of slavery, and in the years ahead would clamor noisily for its "reannexation."

When Mexico won its independence in 1821, it inherited from Spain not only an empire in decay, but a deep suspicion of American territorial ambitions. The United States lost little time in confirming these fears. Hoping to take advantage of the new nation's serious financial difficulties in the wake of its decade-long revolutionary struggle, Washington offered to buy Texas, but its efforts served only to sour relations between the two countries. Diplomats sent by the administrations of John Quincy Adams and Andrew Jackson to pursue these negotiations bungled the job, badgering Mexican leaders and creating much anti-American feeling. Resentful and defiant, the Mexican government regarded the nation's territorial integrity as a point of honor that could not be compromised.

While fending off overtures from the United States to part with a large portion of the national domain, Mexican leaders fought among themselves, deeply divided over how to build a post-colonial republic. Liberal federalists advocated a decentralized system of government not unlike that of the United States, favoring considerable regional autonomy for their far-flung empire. Conservative centralists, on the other hand, viewed Mexico City as the nation's political and cultural epicenter. Drawing much of their support from such entrenched bastions of privilege as the church and the army, they had been among the last to support the cause of independence, subscribing to an authoritarian model of government that owed more to Spanish colonial rule than to Jeffersonian republicanism.

Weakened by factionalism and chronic political instability, Mexico was unable to prevent Anglo-Americans in Texas from fomenting revolution and declaring independence in 1836. Although the United States officially assumed a neutral posture during the conflict, the revolt could not have succeeded without the active participation of American citizens, many of whom were soldiers of fortune from the southeastern United States attracted by land bounties offered by the rebel government. A U.S. army on the Texas–Louisiana border had briefly crossed the Sabine River at the height of the crisis, leading Mexicans to charge that the United States would have intervened militarily had events not gone the Texans' way. As a result, even though the United States refrained from annexing Texas after San Jacinto, Mexicans remained convinced that the Revolution was little more than a brazen land grab, the culmination of a plot by Anglo-Americans to seize by conquest what they could not gain by legitimate means.

The Texas Revolution was a traumatic experience for Mexico, a stain on the nation's honor that federalists and centralists alike vowed to erase. There was much more than national pride at stake. Mexican leaders believed, not unreasonably, that the loss of Texas would only whet the American appetite for more land. Thus Mexico refused to recognize Texas independence, clinging instead to the fiction that its former province was in a state of rebellion. Any attempt by the United States to acquire Texas, Mexico declared, would be a violation of its territorial sovereignty and would constitute an act of war.

As the years passed, however, Mexican leaders, faced with a bankrupt treasury, were unable to make good on their promises of reconquest. Twice in 1842 the Mexican government had dispatched troops to seize San Antonio, announcing that these forays were the vanguard of a full-scale invasion. But the campaign to regain Texas never occurred, and the following year Texas and American diplomats reopened annexation talks. For all intents and purposes, Mexico now found itself in the humiliating position of a forlorn bystander, its threats of dire consequences brushed aside as the United States and Texas moved closer to an agreement of union.

When Congress passed the joint resolution offering to annex the Texas Republic in early March 1845, it bequeathed to Polk the first crisis of his administration. On March 6, two days after the inauguration, Mexico's minister in Washington asked for his passports and sailed for home, thus severing diplomatic relations between his country and the United States. Ominous as these developments seemed, Mexico's president, José Joaquín Herrera, was anxious to avoid a conflict with Washington. Though he continued to look for ways to block annexation, he was equally determined to resist the demands of conservatives who insisted that only a war could redeem the nation's honor. In this policy, the Mexican government had the firm support of Great Britain, which likewise opposed a union between the two Anglo-American republics. Troubled by the rise of the United States as a hemispheric power, British Foreign Secretary Lord Aberdeen viewed a free and independent Texas as an impediment to American continental ambitions. In addition, Texas promised to develop into a rich source of cotton, which would lessen British dependence on the United States for the commodity, so vital to Britain's thriving textile industry.

Finally, after a period of indecision and some prodding by the British, the Mexican government moved to prevent the impending marriage between the United States and Texas. Abandoning the untenable position that Texas was still a province in revolt, the Herrera regime reluctantly offered to recognize the Republic as a sovereign nation— but only if it would promise to reject annexation to the United States. Texas president Anson Jones, who was not averse to keeping his options open, agreed to present the idea to the voters of Texas, and in the early summer of 1845 there appeared to be a possibility—albeit a slim one—that the Republic might reject the offer of annexation now being tendered by the United States.

Polk was determined to thwart this 11th-hour bid to block annexation, convinced that Great Britain intended to make Texas "a dependency of her own." The Texas Republic represented the holy grail to the expansionist crusade; to lose it now after so long a quest was unthinkable. U.S. chargé d'affaires to the Republic Andrew Jackson Donelson—a nephew of the former president—and other agents sent by the Polk administration to keep an eye on events in Texas contributed to the crisis atmosphere. Washington received breathless reports from Donelson that Mexico, urged on by the British, planned to invade Texas if annexation was consummated. According to the U.S. diplomat, who shared with Polk a deep suspicion of British intentions, Mexico's decision to recognize Texas at this late stage was merely "a contrivance of Great Britain" designed to inflame tensions between the neighboring countries. Her Majesty's government had engineered the Mexican peace overture with the knowledge that its rejection by the people of Texas would be interpreted as a hostile act by Mexican leaders, the U.S. chargé d'affaires believed. Having failed repeatedly in its attempts to block annexation, Great Britain now intended to goad Mexico into a conflict with the United States.

Donelson's fears had little basis in fact. Far from encouraging Mexico to embark on a war against its northern neighbors, Her Majesty's government had warned Mexico that it could expect no aid from Great Britain should it invade Texas. Long-time residents of Texas had learned to take rumors of Mexican troop movements below the Rio Grande with a hefty dose of skepticism; in the past such threats had proven to be nothing more than empty saber rattling on the part of Mexican leaders, designed primarily to shore up political support at home. Nonetheless, Donelson prevailed on Texas leaders to accept U.S. military protection, and on June 15 the War Department ordered General Zachary Taylor, commander of a force of 1,500 men stationed in western Louisiana, to move to the Texas frontier. On the same day, Polk took the added precaution of ordering an American naval build-up in the Gulf of Mexico. When Taylor and his troops arrived in Texas by land and sea routes at the end of July, Donelson instructed them to take up position at Corpus Christi, on the south bank of the Nueces River.

With the decision to station U.S. troops below the Nueces, the crisis between the United States and Mexico entered a new and dangerous phase. Claimed both by Mexico and Texas, the land between the Nueces and the Rio Grande was disputed territory. Mexico recognized the Nueces River as the boundary of Texas, while the Republic claimed the Rio Grande, 130 miles farther south, as the dividing line between the two countries. By ordering Taylor into the trans-Nueces, the administration served notice that it intended to uphold the Texas boundary claim, a position that Mexican conservatives regarded as grounds for war.

The Texans' claim to the region was flimsy at best. The Nueces River had served as the boundary of Texas under Spanish and Mexican rule; even as late as 1835, land grant maps drafted by Anglo-American settlers recognized the Nueces, not the Rio Grande, as the legitimate boundary of Texas. As a prisoner after the battle of San Jacinto, Mexican president Antonio López de Santa Anna had accepted the Rio Grande boundary in a secret provision of the treaty ending the Revolution, but the agreement was promptly rejected by the Mexican government. Not to be denied, the Texas Congress simply passed a law in 1836 unilaterally declaring the river to be its southern and western boundary. Since that time, however, it had made virtually no effort to extend its jurisdiction over the territory below the Nueces. During the nine years Texas existed as a republic, the Mexican population of the trans-Nueces region—there were no Anglos to speak of save for a few cattle rustlers—had been governed by Mexican officials and subject to Mexican laws.

While Texas imperialists brashly claimed the Rio Grande as the boundary of the Republic, in 1845 many Anglo-Americans familiar with the issue had come to accept the need for compromise. Texas president Anson Jones viewed the trans-Nueces as disputed territory, while the joint resolution of annexation recently passed by the U.S. Congress deliberately avoided any mention of the Texas boundary with Mexico, assuming that the dispute could be resolved at a later date. Even Andrew Jackson Donelson, who had ordered the U.S. Army to take up positions below the Nueces, was at pains to point out that his decision did not constitute an endorsement of the Texas boundary claim and did not rule out the possibility of a negotiated settlement at a later date.

But during the early summer of 1845, Polk was less interested in sorting out which nation had the more valid claim to the region than in presenting the United States as the protector of Texas. Washington aimed to send a clear and unequivocal message to Mexico and Great Britain that it would brook no interference in its plans to annex Texas; it further wished to demonstrate to wavering Texans that it could rely on the United States to defend their interests. "I am resolved to defend and protect Texas as far as I possess the constitutional power to do so," Polk told Donelson. In fact, however, the administration had not only committed itself to the military protection of Texas, but to something far more controversial: the defense of a boundary claim that to many observers seemed both extravagant and unwarranted.

It soon became evident that the administration had little to fear from British and Mexican efforts to derail its annexation plans. The Mexican proposal to recognize the Republic's right to exist had come too late to change the minds of most Texans. Support for a union with the United States had always been strong in Texas and had gained momentum in recent months, as an ever-increasing tide of American citizens poured into the region. In mid-June, the Texas Congress rejected the Mexican offer and unanimously endorsed the American proposal of annexation.

On July 4, a special convention voted to join the United States under the terms provided by the joint resolution the U.S. Congress had passed in March. Once again, Mexico's newspapers thundered and its politicians struck a warlike pose; once again, an invasion of Texas failed to materialize.

Throughout the summer the Polk administration remained vigilant, responding periodically to new rumors of Mexican troop activity below the Rio Grande. On July 30, Secretary of War Marcy ordered General Taylor to "approach as near the boundary line, the Rio Grande, as prudence will dictate." Taylor stayed where he was for the moment while awaiting reinforcements. The following month the administration informed him that any attempt by Mexico to cross the river should be repelled with force.

Despite the administration's ostensibly belligerent posture, Polk did not intend these actions to be construed as a sign of hostile American intentions toward Mexico. On the contrary, Taylor was repeatedly enjoined to remain on the defensive and to take no steps that might provoke a war. Polk never wavered in his belief that a vigorous show of strength was the best way to deal with the threat of aggression. If the Mexican government could be convinced of the administration's unflinching resolve, it would commit no act of war against Texas or the United States. By the fall of 1845, Polk had every reason to think that his policies were working. Mexico had blustered and threatened, but its troops remained below the Rio Grande.

Even as the Polk administration was staking its highly dubious claim to Mexican territory below the Nueces, it was casting covetous eyes toward other lands held by its Latin American neighbor. Like Spain, Mexico had never managed to establish more than a tenuous control over California, its northernmost province. For years the dilapidated presidios that dotted the Pacific coast had been all but abandoned by the government in Mexico City, the hungry soldiers who manned them more of a burden to the local populace than a source of protection. In 1841 U.S. naval commander Charles Wilkes visited the area and found "a total absence of all government in California, and even its forms and ceremonies thrown aside." Separatist revolts had become commonplace, the latest of which in December 1844 unseated the provincial governor and established an autonomous government.

For American expansionists, the acquisition of California had not been an issue in the 1844 presidential campaign, and up to this point had elicited little attention in the national press. Preoccupied by more immediate territorial issues, imperialist-minded Democrats saw little need for urgency, particularly in view of Mexico's manifest inability to govern the area. In recent years, a few hundred settlers from the United States had trickled into the San Joaquin valley, leading expansionists to predict that California would follow the pattern established in Texas and now evident in Oregon, extending American dominion by gradual, peaceful settlement.

As the crisis with Mexico became more heated, however, Polk was no longer willing to take a passive role. In June, the administration sent secret instructions to Commodore John D. Sloat, commander of the Pacific Fleet, ordering him to remain on alert and instructing him to seize the port of San Francisco and other strategic points along the coast if war broke out. Since these ports were of little practical military value in a war between the United States and Mexico, it seems clear that Polk was already looking ahead to the territorial concessions that might be won in the event of an American victory. While these orders do not prove that the president was willing to provoke a conflict with Mexico to gain California, he seems to have thought it advisable to draft a contingency plan if one occurred; well aware of that region's potential value to the United

States, he would not hesitate to seize and hold it as spoils of war should Mexico initiate hostilities.

As in the case of its Texas policy, the administration's course in California was shaped by misinformation and rumor. And, again as in the case of Texas, Washington saw the hand of the British working actively to thwart its territorial objectives. No sooner had the furor over annexation died down than the expansionist press began to paint grim scenarios of British meddling in California. According to one unfounded rumor, the British were attempting to purchase the territory, offering as payment the assumption of Mexico's debt obligations to British creditors. Particularly alarming to the administration was the letter it received on October 11 from Thomas Larkin, the U.S. consul in Monterey and a devoted propagandist for American expansion in California. Larkin claimed, among other things, that the British were financing a military expedition to suppress the new California government and bring it back under Mexican control. Information from other American agents in the days that followed seemed to lend credence to such reports. Suddenly apprehensive, Washington began to regard California as a matter requiring its immediate attention.

While the Polk administration was mulling its options as it contemplated adding California to its territorial agenda, encouraging developments in Mexico City promised to defuse tensions between the two countries. Acting on the instructions of Secretary of State Buchanan, U.S. consul John Black had met in October with Herrera's foreign minister to ascertain if Mexico would agree to receive an envoy with the authority "to adjust all questions between the two governments." To this request, Foreign Minister Peña y Peña responded in the affirmative, stating that his government wished "to settle the present dispute in a peaceful, reasonable and honorable manner." With these meetings, the groundwork for productive negotiations between the two countries appeared to have been laid. Assuming that Mexico was now prepared to restore normal diplomatic relations, the president on November 10 appointed John Mason Slidell, a Louisiana attorney who was fluent in Spanish, as U.S. minister to Mexico.

In fact, however, Black and Peña y Peña had agreed to two very different things. The Herrera government had expressed a willingness to discuss only "the present dispute," that is, the Texas question. Since this matter would first have to be resolved before normal diplomatic intercourse between the two countries could be restored, it assumed the Polk administration would send a commissioner empowered to settle Mexico's grievances regarding the loss of its former province. Only then could Mexico receive a U.S. minister and resume regular diplomatic relations.

The distinction was by no means an insignificant one. Having failed to prevent annexation, the Herrera regime was now prepared to work toward a new, face-saving objective: a negotiated settlement with the United States that would include compensation for Texas. For the Mexican government it was imperative, therefore, that normal diplomatic relations be withheld until after a settlement had been reached. To receive a U.S. minister at this stage would, in effect, signal Mexico's acceptance of annexation, an impossible negotiating position. Equally important, the reopening of full diplomatic relations would be interpreted by Mexican conservatives as an intolerable sign of weakness, raising a public outcry that the already fragile government could not be expected to survive.

Whether Polk's decision to send a minister instead of a commissioner to Mexico was a simple misunderstanding or a deliberate misreading of the Herrera government's request is open to question. At any rate, the administration's instructions to Slidell removed all doubt that Washington was unsympathetic to Mexico's concerns. While the Herrera government regarded annexation as the principal cause of friction between the two countries, Polk declined even to give his diplomat the authority to discuss the issue. Since the Republic had existed for almost a decade as a sovereign nation, and had now chosen to enter the Union of its own accord, the president believed Mexico had no just cause for complaint.

Polk was equally unwilling to concede that Mexico had a valid claim to the trans-Nueces. On this point he was prepared to be more conciliatory, however, for he regarded the boundary dispute to be the principal obstacle to normal diplomatic relations between the United States and Mexico. To obtain the Herrera government's recognition of the Rio Grande as the boundary of Texas, the president offered to assume payment of American claims against the Mexican government totaling $3.25 million.

The claims issue had soured relations between the two countries for several years. A sizable American and European business community had operated in Mexico since its independence, attracted by the opportunities for high profits, while at the same time insisting on protection from the hazards of doing business in a politically unstable country. As the Mexican economy deteriorated, prosperous foreign merchants had often become targets of popular rage, incurring sizable losses for which they held the Mexican government responsible. While American diplomats admitted that the damage claims submitted by American citizens were frequently exaggerated, the United States government demanded payment, threatening military action in 1837 to enforce collection. Mexico agreed to a payment schedule in 1843, but mounting debts had forced it to stop payment on further installments a year later.

Slidell's mission would have been ambitious enough had it been limited to a satisfactory resolution of the claims problem and the Texas boundary dispute, issues that had been both contentious and of long standing. But the Polk administration believed the time was ripe to pressure Mexico into making further concessions. Alarmed by reports of British interference in California, Polk instructed Slidell to warn Mexican leaders that the United States would take steps to prevent the cession of California to any European power. Should Mexico wish to sell this land, however, the United States was prepared to make several propositions. For the New Mexico territory, the American envoy was authorized to offer the Herrera government $5 million. The administration was also willing to pay $20 million for northern California and would raise the price to $25 million for a territorial cession that included the Pacific ports of San Francisco and Monterey.

Slidell's mission, then, as conceived by the president and members of his cabinet, sought to address several issues crucial to American hemispheric interests. Buchanan did not exaggerate when he observed that the mission entrusted to the new envoy to Mexico was "one of the most delicate and important which has ever been confided to a citizen of the United States." No doubt the president believed that Mexico, given its impecunious condition, would have little choice but to accept the U.S. offer. So convinced was Polk that his diplomatic gambit would soon be crowned with success that he confidently wrote to his younger brother William: "There will be no war with Mexico."

Given the wellspring of resentment toward the United States in Mexico, such optimism was at the very least premature. The Mexican government could hardly be expected to respond favorably to Washington's insistence that it accept the loss of Texas without apology or compensation. Nor could the Herrera regime possibly consider the sale of California and New Mexico, an offer that Mexican patriots would regard as nothing less than an invitation to participate in the dismemberment of the national domain. To even entertain the suggestion of additional cessions to the United States would be an act of political suicide for the beleaguered government, already denounced by conservatives for its inability to prevent the annexation of Texas.

Polk seems to have given little if any thought to how Slidell's diplomatic errand might be received in Mexico. The president believed that war would not be averted by conciliatory gestures on the part of the United States, but by the vigorous application of consistent pressure on the Mexican government until it bowed to American demands. As long as the United States continued to negotiate from a position of strength, it need not concern itself too much with the bruised feelings of Mexican leaders. At no time, in private or public, did the president employ the racist language so common among Americans of his day when discussing the crisis with Mexico. Rather, Polk's contempt for its people and its government was revealed in what he did *not* say. The president held Mexican leaders in such low esteem that he framed his foreign policy without regard for what they might do. Armed with a self-righteousness that made it difficult for him to appreciate contrary opinions, even among those who shared his cultural background, Polk was singularly ill-equipped to understand a foreign adversary. Never would the president's inability to peer beyond the breastworks of a well-guarded world view be more evident, or lead to more fateful consequences.

In the midst of this crisis with Mexico, the Polk administration was about to reach a dangerous impasse with a far more powerful opponent for control of another part of the hemisphere. A dispute between the United States and Great Britain over ownership of the Oregon territory had been brewing for some time. British and American naval expeditions both claimed to have discovered the area in the late eighteenth century. Prior to the War of 1812, trading companies from both countries vied for the lucrative fur trade, buying pelts from the Indians that were then shipped to the Orient, where they could be sold for huge profits. By far the most successful of these operations was the British-owned Hudson's Bay Company, which built a fort at the mouth of the Columbia River and a chain of outposts throughout the Pacific Northwest.

In 1818, British and American diplomats agreed to the joint occupation of the region, an agreement that was renewed in 1827. With Americans largely ignorant of the potential attractions of Oregon, however, the Hudson's Bay Company enjoyed virtual control over the region. This situation changed in 1834, when American missionaries settled in the fertile Willamette Valley. Due largely to their efforts to promote the area in the United States, hundreds of land-hungry settlers were soon making their way along the Oregon Trail. By the mid–1840s, some 5,000 emigrants had made the trek across the continent.

Negotiations between the United States and Great Britain for a permanent settlement of the Oregon question were already well underway when Polk took office. The Tyler administration had suggested dividing the Oregon territory roughly in half at the 49th parallel; the British responded with an offer to establish the boundary at the Columbia River, which flowed, for the most part, well south of the 49° line. Although substantial differences remained, the two nations appeared to be inching slowly toward an amicable solution.

By 1844, however, a spirit of compromise was noticeably absent among American expansionists. With public interest in the Oregon territory on the rise, they began to take a much more aggressive posture in asserting U.S. claims in the Pacific Northwest. Recent naval intelligence revealed that a sand bar at the mouth of the Columbia made the harbor a poor port of call for American ships; the harbors of the Puget Sound to the north, expansionists now argued, offered an infinitely more attractive gateway to Asian commerce. Eager to attract new groups to the Manifest Destiny crusade, the Democrats nailed an "All Oregon" plank onto their campaign platform in 1844, claiming the entire region for the United States up to the 54°40' line.

Many Whigs—and not a few Democrats—feared that the bellicose demand for "All Oregon" would plunge the United States into a war with Great Britain, the world's leading naval power. The Democrats' campaign pledge was particularly unpopular in the Northeast and Deep South, regions that feared the disruption of normal trade relations with Great Britain. John C. Calhoun, having presided over the Oregon negotiations with Great Britain as Tyler's secretary of state, advised a policy of inaction. With American settlement in the region rapidly increasing, and the Hudson's Bay Company's activities in the area expected to diminish as the fur-bearing animal population declined, the United States had little to gain by forcing the issue. Time, Calhoun and others argued, was on the side of the United States.

Those who hoped that the new administration would abandon its campaign bluster and endeavor to reach a compromise with Great Britain over the Oregon territory could not have been heartened by Polk's inaugural address, in which he reiterated the Democratic campaign position that the American claim to Oregon was "clear and unquestionable." Polk's bold stand on behalf of American territorial ambitions was not mere gasconade, nor was it a pose to satisfy western expansionists—he genuinely believed that the United States possessed a valid claim to the entire territory. This did not mean, however, that Polk was prepared to go to war with Great Britain if American demands were not met. The president's uncompromising position was intended to pressure the British government into a quick resolution of the problem, but he was prepared to yield if necessary. As in his posture toward Mexico, Polk believed that tough talk was the only language the nation's hemispheric rivals understood.

In July 1845, Polk sought to reopen negotiations with Great Britain on the Oregon question. While continuing to defend its claim for all of Oregon, the administration offered, as Tyler had done, to divide the territory at the 49th parallel. In his instructions to Louis McLane, the new U.S. minister to the Court of St. James, Secretary of State Buchanan suggested that the administration might be willing to cede a small portion of Vancouver Island to the British, and later instructed McLane to offer all of the island if it might bring the negotiations to a speedy conclusion. But while the proposal represented a marked retreat from the administration's initial hard-line position, Polk was not quite ready to go as far as his predecessor. The new administration refused to grant the British navigation rights on the Columbia River, a negotiating point the Tyler government had already conceded. At any rate, Polk's offer was intended as a basis for further discussions and was not to be construed by British diplomats as Washington's final word on the subject.

Even before they could begin, the negotiations were brought to an abrupt halt by Sir Richard Pakenham, Britain's minister in Washington, who had also received a copy of the administration's proposal. In view of the fact that the British Foreign Office had rejected a more advantageous settlement in its negotiations with the Tyler administration one year earlier, Pakenham assumed that the new U.S. proposal would be totally unacceptable to Her Majesty's government. Acting on his own authority, Pakenham peremptorily rejected Buchanan's offer before his superiors in Whitehall had a chance to respond to this new diplomatic initiative from Washington.

Bristling at the rebuff, which he assumed had been issued on orders from Lord Aberdeen, the British foreign secretary, Polk ordered Buchanan to withdraw the offer. Privately, the president may have welcomed the impasse, aware that his willingness to compromise had angered the 54°40' men. Convinced that any further entreaties on the part of the United States would be seen as a sign of weakness, Polk decided to slam the door shut on further negotiations.

Secretary of State James Buchanan was alarmed by the president's intransigence. With Mexico threatening to go to war over Texas, Buchanan believed that this was no time to antagonize the British. By seeking to deny Great Britain an outlet on the Pacific Ocean, the administration might well push Her Majesty's government into an alliance with Mexico. When the cabinet discussed how best to respond to the Pakenham letter in a meeting on August 26, Buchanan fairly begged the president to leave open the possibility of further negotiations. The secretary of state suggested that the administration's official reply might contain a paragraph inviting the British to make a counter-offer to the U.S. proposal, but Polk, believing his initial offer had been eminently fair and reasonable, gave the idea short shrift. When Buchanan remarked that the administration's reply to Britain should at least be postponed until it could be known whether there would be a war with Mexico, Polk replied that he "saw no necessary connection between the two questions," adding that "we should do our duty towards both Mexico and Great Britain and firmly maintain our rights, and leave the rest to God and the country." Such fatalism was of little comfort to the cautious Buchanan, who could only grumble in reply that "God would not have much to do in justifying us in a war for the country north of 49."

Fortunately for Polk, the British were anxious to come to some sort of accommodation with the United States. While prepared to defend its claim to northern Oregon, Her Majesty's government was very much aware of the economic advantages of peace. With the annexation of Texas imminent, the United States enjoyed a virtual monopoly of cotton production, while the famine in Ireland had increased Britain's dependence on American wheat. Moreover, Polk's efforts to pass a free trade bill were being followed with great interest among British manufacturers, who were looking forward to greater access to lucrative American markets.

For these reasons, Lord Aberdeen moved quickly to try to undo the damage Pakenham had caused. The foreign secretary censured his hapless minister in Washington and informed him that he had not been speaking for Her Majesty's government when he rejected the U.S. proposal. On Aberdeen's instructions, a chagrined Pakenham formally withdrew the letter that had brought about the diplomatic impasse. Once interrupted, however, the dialogue between the United States and Great Britain could not be easily restored. Ever suspicious of British motives, Polk remained decidedly cool toward further negotiations, adamantly refusing to resubmit the offer Pakenham had so rashly rejected. If Great Britain wished to make an offer of its own, he allowed grudgingly after much prodding from Buchanan, the United States would receive it, but Polk refused to give any assurances that such an offer would receive serious consideration. Thus while Buchanan labored to keep relations between the two countries on an even keel, Polk seemed bent on scuttling them.

On December 2, Polk's private secretary Joseph Knox Walker delivered a copy of the president's first annual message to Capitol Hill, where it was read to both houses of Congress. With characteristic thoroughness, Polk had begun his initial draft of the message—the first major policy paper of his presidency—two months earlier. The document had gone through countless revisions, with the president working closely with members of his cabinet and soliciting the advice of congressional leaders. But the message to Congress was a collaborative enterprise only up to a point, and in its final form bore the unmistakable imprint of the strong-willed chief executive. While the document contained none of the hyperbole of the jingoistic press, it offered the clearest exposition yet of the president's expansionist creed. Revealing the underlying fear of Europe that fueled the Manifest Destiny movement, Polk reaffirmed in precise, colorless prose the government's commitment to the Monroe Doctrine, declaring that "no future European colony or dominion shall with our consent be planted or established on any part of the North American continent."

By far the most eagerly awaited portion of the president's message dealt with the Oregon question. In a move that was widely viewed as an ominous first step toward hostilities with Great Britain, Polk called on Congress to end the joint occupation of Oregon and assume full control of the territory, British claims to the region notwithstanding. "All attempts at compromise having failed," the president asked that Congress give Her Majesty's government a year's notice before terminating the joint occupation treaty, as the agreement required. Polk also urged that appropriate measures be taken to ensure the safety of American citizens in Oregon and proposed that forts be built along the Oregon Trail to protect emigrants. He further suggested that Congress enact a liberal land policy to stimulate American settlement once joint occupation formally ended.

So great was the public interest in the Oregon issue that the president's comments regarding relations with Mexico passed almost unnoticed. The annexation of Texas, Polk declared, had been "a bloodless achievement" that had occurred despite "the diplomatic interference of European monarchies." Sidestepping the Mexican claim to the trans-Nueces, Polk stated blandly that American dominion had been "peacefully extended to the [Rio Grande] del Norte."

Although the president's message was widely praised by Democrats across the country, there could be no denying that the administration's bellicose posturing had placed the nation in an extremely difficult position. While Polk did not want war with Great Britain or Mexico, he had gone out of his way to antagonize them, pursuing an aggressive foreign policy that made a war with one or both nations a very real possibility.

Thus an extraordinary picture presented itself as the year 1845 drew to a close. While the administration steadfastly maintained a pose of aggrieved innocence, it had dispatched American troops to take up positions on territory claimed by Mexico and called on Congress to completely disregard long-respected British claims in the Pacific Northwest. Desolate and devoid of population, both the trans-Nueces and the land above the 49th parallel in Oregon offered scant prospect of near-term economic development and could hardly be considered vital to U.S. security interests. The American title to both regions, moreover, rested on feeble if not wholly indefensible grounds. Observers of the international scene might well have wondered if the policy of brinkmanship so aggressively pursued by the administration was merely a bluff, or if Polk was really prepared to go to war to defend these claims. The answer to that question would be revealed in the months ahead.

8

"Hostilities Have Commenced"

Facing crises on twin fronts and viewing the deteriorating situation with Great Britain as the greater danger of the two, the administration was anxious to resolve its problems with Mexico as quickly as possible. The disturbing reports of British activities in California added to the sense of urgency in Washington. To hasten the reopening of diplomatic relations with Mexico, Polk took the unorthodox step of sending John Slidell on his diplomatic mission without waiting for the Senate to confirm his appointment. To save even more time, the new American envoy was ordered to sail from his home in New Orleans to Pensacola, Florida, where his instructions were waiting for him, and then to proceed immediately to Mexico. On November 29, Slidell disembarked at Veracruz, barely six weeks after John Black, the U.S. consul in Mexico City, and Mexican foreign minister Manuel Peña y Peña had met to discuss the reopening of diplomatic channels.

Slidell's arrival caught the Herrera regime completely off-guard. Assuming that a U.S. envoy would not be named until the U.S. Congress convened in December, the Mexican government did not expect Slidell to arrive until early the following year. Peña y Peña had not yet had time to build support in the Mexican Congress and in the state legislatures for the regime's decision to open a dialogue with the

United States. To make matters worse for the Herrera government, it was rumored in the Mexican press that Slidell had been authorized to discuss not only the annexation of Texas and the boundary dispute, but also the purchase of California. Opposition newspapers were quick to accuse Herrera of selling out to the United States. The headline of one newspaper screamed: "The Treason has been Discovered!"

In fact, Slidell's instructions were already out of date, for the administration had ceased to regard California as a top priority. Polk's readiness to take an active role in the acquisition of ports on the Pacific waxed and waned in direct proportion to his fear of British activities in the region. Thus when another dispatch from U.S. consul Thomas Larkin in California arrived in early December, seeming to indicate that the area was in no immediate danger from the British, the president ordered Secretary of State Buchanan to modify his instructions to Slidell. If Mexican leaders showed no interest in selling California, the American envoy was told, he should not allow the issue to upset the chances for normalizing relations between the two countries.

But the damage to the Herrera regime had already been done. The Mexican government found itself in a predicament that was as awkward as it was precarious; having requested a U.S. envoy, it could not receive him without provoking a revolution. The tottering government gave Slidell a less than enthusiastic welcome when he arrived in Mexico City. Playing for time in hopes that the public furor might die down, Peña y Peña declined to accept Slidell's credentials on the grounds that Mexico had agreed only to receive a commissioner empowered to settle existing grievances, not a minister plenipotentiary. He urged Slidell to write to Washington to obtain new credentials.

The U.S. envoy politely but firmly declined the Mexican foreign minister's request. In his letters to Secretary of

State Buchanan, however, Slidell seethed with indignation at what he perceived to be Mexican foot dragging and "absurd" squabbling over matters of protocol. Like many American diplomats during the Jacksonian period, Slidell possessed a haughty disregard for cultures different from his own. Viewing the Mexican people as "feeble and degraded," he had little sympathy for the embattled Herrera government, and had already come to the conclusion that it was too weak to enter into constructive negotiations. Differences between Mexico and the United States "must be settled promptly," Slidell wrote in exasperation to Buchanan, "either by negotiation or the sword."

Slidell's arrival in Mexico sealed the fate of the Herrera regime. In a chain of events that had become all too familiar in Mexico, General Mariano Paredes y Arrillaga, a conservative who had engineered the overthrow of Santa Anna one year earlier, issued a *pronunciamiento* against Herrera on December 15 and marched on the nation's capital. Rather than subject the nation to a bloody civil war on the eve of its greatest crisis with the United States, Herrera resigned and handed over the reins of government to Paredes.

Slidell did not lament the passing of the Herrera regime, taking the view that a new government might be in a stronger position to negotiate with the United States. Once the revolutionary tumult had subsided, the U.S. diplomat withdrew to Jalapa, a town midway between Mexico City and the port city of Veracruz, to await further instructions from Washington and to see if the Paredes government might adopt a different tack toward a possible diplomatic settlement with the United States.

The U.S. minister's new hopes for the success of his mission soon proved groundless. A man of strong anti-American sentiments, Paredes showed little interest in reaching an accord with the United States. Instead, the conservative military leader became involved in a plot hatched by Spanish officials to return Mexico to Bourbon monarchical rule, a scheme that had little public support and merely added to the confusion of an already chaotic political scene. Despite the strident anti-American posture Paredes assumed on seizing power, like his predecessors he temporized, while the press inveighed against American aggression and cried for war.

The administration took a predictably hard line when it learned in mid-January of Mexico's rejection of Slidell. Secretary of State Buchanan wrote to the U.S. envoy ordering him to demand his passports and return home if Mexico did not abandon its position and recognize his credentials as a diplomatic representative of the United States. Should Mexico refuse to receive him, Buchanan noted ominously, "the cup of forbearance will then have been exhausted. Nothing can remain but to take the redress of the injuries to our citizens and the insults to our Government into our own hands."

Meanwhile, Polk turned up the heat on Mexico by ordering Zachary Taylor once again to move his army to the Rio Grande. Having now received the reinforcements he had been waiting for, Taylor broke camp and marched south at the head of an army numbering almost 4,000. Arriving in late March 1846, Taylor erected fortifications across the river from Matamoros, where his cannons could direct their fire into the plaza of the Mexican town, while U.S. gunships blockaded the mouth of the river. Not everyone in Taylor's army was anxious for battle. "We have not one particle of right to be here," lamented the New England-born Colonel Ethan Allen Hitchcock.

Despite—or perhaps because of—these threatening maneuvers, Polk remained sanguine that war could be averted, and that Mexico would ultimately come to terms. The president had, in fact, already received assurances to that effect from an unlikely source. In February, Polk had been visited at the White House by Alexander Atocha, a confidant of former Mexican president Santa Anna who, though living comfortably in exile in Havana, remained a figure to be reckoned with in Mexican politics. Atocha explained that the Mexican general was planning to regain power, and if successful was prepared to reach a negotiated settlement with Washington. For $30 million, Santa Anna offered to cede California and New Mexico to the United States. Though Polk's interest was clearly piqued, he declined to pursue these overtures, at least for the time being. The American president had little faith in Atocha or the man he claimed to represent, and in any case he could do nothing until he learned the fate of Slidell's diplomatic mission. Nonetheless, Atocha's visit confirmed for Polk what he had long believed: that Mexican leaders would much rather sell off large parcels of land to the United States than undertake a costly and quixotic war.

Although the president was not yet ready to cooperate in the intrigues of the exiled Santa Anna, the administration did seek to capitalize on the political turmoil in Mexico City in other ways. On March 12, 1846, Secretary of State Buchanan ordered Slidell to return to Mexico City and once again press his demand to be received as U.S. minister by the new Paredes government. Mindful of Mexico's financial troubles, Polk suggested in a cabinet meeting a few days later that the administration ask Congress to appropriate a special $1 million discretionary fund which could be placed at Slidell's disposal. Knowing that Paredes was in dire need of cash to pay the army, on which the survival of his new regime depended, Polk reasoned that Slidell could use the money to induce the Mexican government to sign a treaty with the United States.

But the time for negotiations had passed. Acting on his earlier instructions, Slidell had delivered an ultimatum to the Mexican government on March 1, demanding that Mexico receive him as minister within the next two weeks. Twelve days later he received his reply from the Paredes government: Mexico would not negotiate with an army encamped on its soil and a navy anchored off its shores. His patience with what he regarded as Mexican effrontery at an end, Slidell demanded his passports and sailed for home. "Depend upon it," the U.S. envoy angrily wrote to Secretary of State Buchanan, "we can never get along well with [the Mexicans], until we have given them a good drubbing." With Slidell's departure, all hope of a constructive dialogue between the United States and Mexico came to an end.

As the country moved closer to a showdown with Mexico, the administration gave no sign of softening its belligerent attitude toward Great Britain. Following up on the tough talk of his December presidential message, Polk forged ahead with his plan to persuade Congress to terminate the joint occupation agreement in the early months of 1846. An offer by British minister Richard Pakenham in January to submit the Oregon dispute to international arbitration was flatly rejected by the administration. Polk remained convinced, as he told a South Carolina congressman, that "the only way to treat John Bull is to look him straight in the eye . . . ." As in his dealings with Mexico, Polk believed that "a bold & firm course on our part [was] the pacific one; that if Congress faultered [sic] or hesitated in their course, John Bull would immediately become more arrogant and more grasping in his demands."

Such blunt, uncompromising talk from the president was just what western expansionists wanted to hear, but many in Congress worried that the administration might be pushing "John Bull" too far. Polk encountered stiff resistance to the termination notice resolution from a disparate coalition of northern and southern legislators who feared that a war with Great Britain would result. Consequently, the House passed a mildly worded resolution that called for an "amicable settlement" of the dispute between the two countries, while moderates in the Senate succeeded in postponing a vote on the measure for several months.

Polk also may have wondered if he had pushed the British too far when he received word in February from Louis McLane, the U.S. minister in London, that a fleet of 30 British warships was preparing to set sail for Canada. The president immediately conferred with his cabinet, and within days new instructions for the U.S. minister were en route to London. McLane was authorized to inform British diplomats that the administration would once again be amenable to a compromise boundary at the 49th parallel, plus limited access to the Columbia River, if they would make such an offer. Though pleased by the administration's sudden willingness to defuse tensions, Lord Aberdeen decided to wait until the Senate voted on the termination notice before taking further action.

During the spring of 1846 the administration appeared to be much more receptive to a negotiated settlement, although in typically inscrutable fashion the president continued to keep congressional leaders guessing as to his real intentions. By the time the Senate finally voted on the termination resolution notice in mid-April, the mood in Washington was clearly one of compromise, which the president, now seeking to distance himself from the 54°40' extremists, did nothing to discourage.

In Mexico, meanwhile, public anger toward the United States was reaching a fever pitch. Centralists and federalists alike called for war against the hated *norteamericanos* that, they argued, would unite the country as never before. Militarists saw war as an opportunity to revitalize the army, long corrupted by factionalism and political intrigue. Inclined to discount the United States as a serious threat, they pointed to the refusal of New York soldiers to march into Canada in the War of 1812 as evidence that American militiamen could not successfully invade foreign soil. Finally, a feeling of desperate rage, the culmination of a series of perceived indignities and insults at the hands of the United States spanning two decades, impelled Mexican leaders down the path toward war.

Slidell arrived in Washington, D.C., during the first week in May. Still chafing at his rebuff by the Mexican government, the diplomat briefed the president on the failure of his mission to Mexico on May 8. Both men agreed that the time had come for the United States "to take the redress of the wrongs and injuries which we have so long borne from Mexico into our own hands . . . ." The following day, May 9, Polk discussed the situation with members of his cabinet. Despite the absence of aggression on the part of Mexico, Polk now believed that its refusal to receive Slidell gave the United States "ample cause of war" and favored sending Congress a declaration to that effect. All cabinet members agreed except George Bancroft, who advised the president to wait until some act of provocation by Mexico.

In fact, the pretext for war that Bancroft sought had already occurred. At 6 P.M. that same evening, Polk received dispatches from General Taylor, notifying him that the Mexican army had crossed the Rio Grande, attacking a patrol of 63 dragoons on April 25. Sixteen Americans were killed and wounded in the exchange, and the rest captured. Taylor's note read: "Hostilities may now be considered as commenced."

Polk hastily summoned his advisers to meet for the second time that day. At 7:30 the cabinet reassembled, with Bancroft now joining the others in favoring a declaration of war against Mexico. After the meeting adjourned at 10:00, Polk, Buchanan, and Bancroft began to draft the war message to Congress.

The following day, Bancroft arrived at the White House and helped the president put the finishing touches on his war message. Polk then attended church, after which he spent the rest of the day discussing the crisis with members of Congress who called at the executive residence. That night Polk noted in his diary in rueful if typically understated fashion: "It was a day of great anxiety to me, and I regretted the necessity which had existed to make it necessary for me to spend the Sabbath in the manner I have."

On Monday, May 11, an excited Congress heard the president's war message. "Mexico has passed the boundary of the United States, has invaded our territory and shed American blood on the American soil. She has proclaimed that hostilities have commenced, and the two nations are now at war." Polk listed the "insults" and "injuries" the United States had suffered at the hands of Mexico: its refusal to pay outstanding claims owed to U.S. citizens; its refusal to recognize the U.S. annexation of Texas or the Rio Grande as the legitimate boundary of Texas; its failure to receive John Slidell.

Not everyone in Congress shared the president's indignation. American blood had been spilled, but many leaders of both parties questioned whether it had been shed on American soil. Democratic senators Thomas Hart Benton and John C. Calhoun, though bitter opponents on most of the great issues of their day, were among those who harbored serious doubts about the American claim to the land below the Nueces River. Ironically, by sending Slidell to Mexico with instructions to negotiate for the Rio Grande boundary, the president himself undermined the validity of the American claim. While Polk had consistently sided with Texas in its territorial dispute with Mexico, he had nonetheless offered to compensate the Mexican government if it would agree to cede its claim to the region, and in so doing lent credence to the argument that the trans-Nueces was disputed territory.

Also troubling to many political leaders was the belief that Polk's decision to declare war against Mexico seemed somewhat premature. Notwithstanding the president's efforts to characterize the border skirmish as an invasion, Texas did not appear to be in any imminent danger of a full-scale Mexican offensive. Shots had indeed been fired, but this did not rule out the possibility that a negotiated settlement could still be reached. As John C. Calhoun noted, there was a considerable difference between hostilities and war. But Polk had now rejected diplomacy as an option; the attack on Taylor's troops gave him the pretext for a war he had convinced himself was necessary after the failure of the Slidell mission. The president did not ask Congress to consider other alternatives, but rather to lend its imprimatur to his contention that a state of war existed.

Not surprisingly, the president's war message made no mention of New Mexico and California, though some congressmen already suspected that Polk was intent on manufacturing a war for the sole purpose of seizing these territories. In his own mind, Polk seems to have sincerely believed that his interest in acquiring the American Southwest had nothing to do with the outbreak of hostilities. There can be little doubt, however, that he had already given considerable thought to the territorial concessions that could be obtained by conquest if war broke out. Whether he recognized it or not, the president's eagerness to achieve these goals, once it became clear that they could not be obtained by peaceful means, led him toward the conclusion that a war with Mexico was the only way to resolve the differences that existed between the two countries.

That territorial objectives were of paramount importance for Polk became evident when, on May 13, Buchanan read to the president and the cabinet a draft of a dispatch he intended to send to U.S. ministers overseas. Fearing that a resolution to the Oregon question might be jeopardized by the conflict along the Rio Grande, and that European powers might join with Mexico if they believed the war was being waged for purposes of territorial aggrandizement, the secretary of state sought to allay any fears those governments might have regarding U.S. intentions. In a carefully worded statement on the war's causes, Buchanan argued that while the United States held fast to the position that the Rio Grande was the legitimate boundary between the two belligerents, it did not go to war to obtain California, New Mexico, or any other portion of Mexican territory. When Buchanan had finished, a stunned Polk told him that he found such assurances "unnecessary and improper." The United States had not gone to war for conquest, he said, but that did not mean it could not claim some territorial indemnity to defray the costs of waging war. The president insisted that Buchanan delete any reference to the "no territory" pledge. The war with Mexico was none of Europe's concern, Polk told his secretary of state, and the United States would fight "England or France or all the Powers of Christendom" before he would make such a promise.

The Polk administration and its supporters in Congress moved quickly to capitalize on public anger at the Mexican attack on Taylor's forces, ramming the war bill through the House with limited debate. A move to examine official documents pertaining to the outbreak of hostilities was promptly tabled, preventing opponents from weighing the evidence on which the president based his claim for war. Administration loyalists skillfully added to the bill a preamble restating Polk's position that war existed "by act of the Republic of Mexico," thereby coupling the declaration of war with the measure to vote men and supplies for Taylor's army. Even Whigs who believed the war was unjustified felt compelled to vote in favor of the measure for fear of seeming unpatriotic in a time of national emergency. As a result, the bill passed handily in the House by a vote of 174 to 14, where the dissenting Whigs were led by the aging John Quincy Adams.

In the Senate, a coalition of Whigs and Calhoun Democrats urged their colleagues not to be stampeded into war, to no avail. As in the House, the administration's critics were stymied by their failure to obtain separate votes on the preamble declaring war and the decision to approve money and supplies. A move to postpone consideration of the bill was also defeated. In the spirited debate preceding the vote, several senators rose to condemn the administration for acting precipitately. One Delaware senator declared that the decision to station troops on the banks of the Rio Grande within range of Matamoros was "as much an act of aggression on our part as is a man's pointing a pistol at another's breast." In the end, however, most fell into line behind the administration, mindful of the political risks of voting against the measure. The Senate passed the war bill by a lopsided 40 to 2 margin, with three senators, among them John C. Calhoun, abstaining.

While these dramatic developments were unfolding in Washington, across the Atlantic British diplomats were perusing the Oregon termination notice, which they received on May 15. Since the document bore little resemblance to the uncompromising position taken by the president in his December message, a resolution of the crisis seemed near. Anxious to proceed with the negotiations that had been derailed for more than nine months, Lord Aberdeen had already drafted a new British offer, unaware that the United States had declared war against Mexico. Aberdeen agreed to accept the 49th parallel compromise line, with the stipulation that Vancouver Island remain under British control. In a last-minute effort to ensure an agreement, U.S. minister McLane prevailed on Lord Aberdeen to make one final, important concession: instead of providing for unlimited British access to the Columbia River, the terms of the offer were changed to provide access only to the Hudson's Bay Company. The British proposal was then shipped off to Washington, ten days before the news of the hostilities along the Rio Grande arrived in London.

By the time Polk received the British offer in early June, he was hardly in a position to protest its terms. Although the president was not in all respects satisfied with the British proposal, he knew full well that the war with Mexico had cost the United States any leverage it had enjoyed in its negotiations with Great Britain over Oregon. To insist on further modifications would only delay a negotiated settlement, and quite possibly encourage Great Britain to take advantage of the administration's Mexico crisis and drive a harder bargain. Since any compromise with the British was bound to be unpopular among western Democrats, the president hit on an unorthodox course of action: he would ask the Senate for its advice before making a decision, thereby shifting to that body at least some responsibility for a treaty that fell far short of his "All Oregon" pledge. As was his custom, the president polled his cabinet members on the matter, all of whom approved of his course except Secretary Buchanan.

Having long been the most vocal advocate for compromise with Great Britain, the secretary of state now startled Polk and other members of the cabinet by expressing his opinion that the president should not retreat from his stand on behalf of all of Oregon. Annoyed, the president suspected that his secretary's about-face on the issue was an attempt to curry favor with western expansionists, a key political bloc for Buchanan should he become a presidential candidate in the next election. When asked by Polk to prepare the message to the Senate that would accompany the British proposal, Buchanan declined to do so, offering only to make suggestions if the president would draft a message of his own. In a private meeting between the president and his secretary of state a few days later, Polk's irritation turned to anger when Buchanan again refused to help him draft the message for the Senate. Instead, Buchanan offered to draft his own message, a remark the president interpreted as a deliberate act of defiance. "Do you wish," Polk demanded hotly, "to draw up a paper of your own to make an issue with me?" Buchanan quickly apologized, but it would require a five-hour cabinet meeting the following day to draft a message that was satisfactory to them both. Accordingly, the administration referred the British proposal to the Senate for its advice, while continuing to insist, at least for the record, on the legitimacy of the American claim to the entire Oregon territory.

Once the British proposal was laid before the Senate, it encountered little opposition. With the nation rushing headlong into war with Mexico, few senators were prepared to risk another with Great Britain. On June 12 the Senate passed a resolution accepting the British offer, with only a handful of western expansionists voting to reject the compromise. One week later the Senate ratified a formal treaty with Great Britain by a vote of 41 to 14.

A few disgruntled Democrats could not contain their bitterness with the Oregon compromise and charged that they had been betrayed by the administration. Polk had led the 54°40' men to believe that he would stand by them; he had done much the same thing with Benton and his followers when he had implied that he would support their alternative plan for the annexation of Texas. Some Democratic politicians accused the administration of cowering before Great Britain, a power they regarded as a far greater threat to U.S. security interests than the nation it was now preparing to invade. Declared one Kentucky congressman: "Whilst we bluster and boast over imbecile Mexico, we present the ridiculous attitude of yielding to England what we have asserted to be our just right, 'clear and indispensable,' and find ourselves in the humiliating position of a whipped hound, sneaking to the kennel at the roar of the British lion." Senator William Allen of Ohio objected so strongly to the administration's course that he resigned the chairmanship of the Foreign Relations Committee. But in the final analysis, the controversy surrounding Polk's abandonment of his campaign pledge to obtain all of Oregon proved to be more of a squall than a storm. With new opportunities for federal patronage created by the war with Mexico, most western Democrats were eager to remain on good terms with the administration and kept their displeasure on the Oregon issue to themselves.

Polk himself seemed to derive little satisfaction from the Oregon compromise. Undemonstrative as always, he recorded the Senate vote ratifying the treaty without comment in his diary. Whatever his personal feelings, the president had scored a significant diplomatic coup in his negotiations with Great Britain. If he had employed more bluster than the situation required, he had nonetheless forced the British to accept an agreement on the Oregon question on terms eminently advantageous to the United States. The president could now devote his full attention and the nation's resources to the conflict with Mexico.

In his handling of the crises with Great Britain and Mexico, Polk had pursued two strikingly similar courses of action. In both cases, the administration adopted an aggressive posture, deliberately calculated to escalate tensions rather than minimize them. Operating on the simple conviction that a bold front was the only way to bring Great Britain and Mexico to the bargaining table, the president did not hesitate to assume a belligerent attitude in order to secure American interests.

This is not to say that the administration's intransigence was merely a pose. In his diplomacy as in his private life, Polk's self-image as a man governed by high moral principles required him to disavow any hint of artifice. Even when attempting to gain a tactical advantage over foreign adversaries, Polk steadfastly insisted that he was taking the high ground. Consequently, the president's demand for all of Oregon and a Texas boundary at the Rio Grande were more than bargaining positions; Polk had convinced himself that the American title to these territories was beyond dispute. Such an inflexible attitude left little room for negotiation, thus bringing the Oregon and Texas problems quickly to the point of crisis.

But if the United States had consistently applied a policy of brinkmanship in its relations with both countries, why did it find itself in 1846 at peace with Great Britain and on a collision course with Mexico? Thomas Hart Benton took the view that the United States had deliberately chosen this path "because Great Britain is powerful and Mexico [is] weak." There was more than a kernel of truth in this analysis. For all his stubborn self-righteousness, the president was a pragmatic politician who knew when to retreat from an untenable situation. Such was the case in the Oregon crisis; when faced with the unsettling prospect of war with Great Britain, Washington quickly came to the conclusion that discretion was the better part of valor and abandoned its extreme territorial demands. When its confrontational policies led to an impasse with Mexico, on the other hand, the administration refused to back down. Polk's decision to apply ever-increasing pressure on Mexico was based on the assumption that its leaders lacked both the will and the resources to wage war against the United States. Even now, as the president called for volunteers to meet the national emergency, he continued to dismiss the likelihood of full-scale military confrontation, convinced that Mexican leaders were anxious to avoid a protracted war.

To Benton's terse assessment must be added the observation that the decision for war was not Polk's alone. The United States reached an accommodation with Great Britain and went to war with Mexico in part because the president's strategy elicited very different responses from the leaders of these countries. Great Britain remained unruffled throughout the Oregon crisis, at times irritated by the administration's intransigence, but never losing sight of the benefits of peace. As the world's reigning naval power, it could well afford to adopt a conciliatory tone, secure in the knowledge that it possessed other options if diplomacy broke down. Mexico's political instability, on the other hand, made it an unpredictable adversary. Polk's bullying tactics only aggravated what was already a highly volatile situation in Mexico City, creating a crisis atmosphere that precluded calm, deliberate policy making on the part of the Mexican government. Instead of intimidating Mexico, the threat of American force had engendered a feeling of desperation and recklessness among its leadership. In the end, retaliation seemed the only recourse to salvage what remained of the nation's honor.

Clearly, the administration had miscalculated. The president was never one to second guess his actions, however, and he saw little reason to do so now. In his mind, responsibility for the crisis could be attributed entirely to Mexican leaders, who had spurned all efforts by the United States to reach a negotiated settlement. Now that war had come, the president faced it with equanimity, his resolve firm, his conscience clear. Supremely confident as to the outcome, he anticipated a short, painless war, one that would enable the United States to obtain the territorial cessions it wanted from Mexico at little cost. As usual, he was certain that he had done the right thing.

9

Mr. Polk's War

James K. Polk was the second American president to declare war. Unlike James Madison during the War of 1812, who lacked both the opportunity and the inclination to exercise the powers of commander-in-chief, Polk from the outset left no doubt as to who was in charge of the war effort. The president determined strategy, chose and replaced officers, and even took a direct role in logistical matters. Nothing in Polk's career had prepared him for the task of planning the nation's first foreign war—he possessed no military training other than the obligatory service in his state militia—yet there is no evidence that he experienced even the slightest anxiety regarding his qualifications for his new role as a war-time chief executive.

With his customary self-assurance, the president developed the broad outlines of a strategy for a campaign against Mexico and submitted them to Secretary of War Marcy and General Winfield Scott. Polk presented his views to the Cabinet two days later in its regular Saturday meeting, which agreed on a two-pronged attack against Mexico. The plan required striking Mexico at two vital points: Santa Fe, New Mexico, in the Southwest and Mexico's northern provinces below the Rio Grande. Two weeks later, Polk proposed adding a third prong to the plan of attack: the outfitting of an expeditionary force to seize Upper California. In addition, U.S. warships, already stationed off the coast of Mexico, received orders to implement a blockade of Veracruz and other principal Mexican ports. Once these objectives were secured, Polk believed, the Mexican government would sue for peace.

While a military strategy was taking shape in Washington, in south Texas the war between U.S. and Mexican forces was already well underway. Emboldened by his troops' initial success against American dragoons, General Mariano Arista, commander of Mexico's Army of the North, crossed the Rio Grande in early May. Arista took up defensive positions at Palo Alto, a waterhole between Fort Brown and Port Isabel, thus cutting General Zachary Taylor off from his base of operations on the Gulf of Mexico. Moving quickly against the Mexican army, Taylor gave the order to attack Arista's troops on the afternoon of May 8. Though heavily outnumbered—perhaps as much as three to one—the American army nonetheless enjoyed enormous advantages in terms of training, equipment, and supplies. Superior American artillery proved decisive in this and subsequent battles of the war, pounding the Mexican ranks with high-explosive shells. Arista retreated, and the following day took up positions a few miles away along a dry river bed at Resaca de la Palma. A frontal assault drove the Mexican army back in some confusion to Matamoros at the mouth of the Rio Grande. As Taylor brought up his heavy mortars in anticipation of a siege, Arista prudently evacuated the town, which U.S. troops occupied on May 18.

Although news of the outbreak of hostilities had provoked a surge of patriotism, a spirit of bipartisanship was noticeably lacking in the nation's capital as the United States prepared for war with Mexico. Troubled by the war itself, many Whigs were equally disturbed by the sweeping new expansion of the federal patronage the crisis had created. The war bill and legislation passed two months later provided for the call-up of volunteers to meet the national emergency. While the task of organizing volunteer troops into battalions and regiments was left to the states, these units were to be organized into brigades and divisions under the auspices of the federal government, and therefore would be led by officers appointed by the commander-in-chief. Within days after the declaration of war, the White House was swarming with congressmen seeking commissions as brigade and division commanders for themselves and their constituents. "The pressure for appointments," Polk noted in his diary on May 21, "is beyond anything of the kind which I have witnessed since I have been President." Despite his disdain for the spoils system, Polk's strong partisan feelings prompted him to grant many of these requests. Initial public enthusiasm for the conflict left the Whigs no choice but to fall into line behind the administration, but privately they watched with dismay and no small amount of envy as the Democrats reaped a rich harvest of military appointments.

Sensitive to the charge that he was using the war to promote his own party's fortunes, the president made a point of reserving some lower-grade commands for Whig partisans, and regularly asked Whig leaders to provide the names of deserving candidates. Such modest efforts, though well intentioned, were not enough to satisfy most Whigs. Nor, for that matter, did Polk's distribution of the federal patronage win the complete approval of his own party. Democratic leaders supported Polk's policy of granting military commissions to Whigs on principle, but not when the appointments were made in volunteer regiments from their own states. A few Democratic congressmen who thirsted for military glory were so angry at being denied commissions that they broke with the administration entirely.

From the earliest days of the war, partisan rancor created an atmosphere of distrust between the administration and the nation's military authorities. While Polk's powers of appointment allowed him to shape the volunteer regimental command structure to suit his purposes, he did not enjoy similar latitude in the professional army, which was top-heavy with Whig partisans in 1846. The highest-ranking officer in the U.S. Army was Winfield Scott, a prominent Whig who had been considered presidential timber by some members of his party even before the war. Although the president had no desire to enhance Scott's political career, he felt he had little choice but to give the country's only major general overall command of the war effort. Polk was not happy with the appointment and disliked the Whig general from the start. "General Scott did not impress me favourably as a military man," Polk recalled after one of their first meetings. "He has had experience in his profession, but I thought was rather scientific and visionary in his views." A vain, overbearing man, Scott might well have given Polk cause for complaint even without their partisan differences. The general was "not averse to speaking of himself, often in the third person," observed a recent West Point graduate named Ulysses S. Grant, "and he could bestow praise upon the person he was talking about without the least embarrassment."

The relationship between the strong-willed president and his commanding general, which began as one of strained cooperation, quickly deteriorated. Insisting on unquestioning obedience from subordinates, Polk was furious to learn that Scott had griped to a senator that the administration intended to appoint western Democrats as officers of a newly created regiment of mounted riflemen (the president, in fact, had already contacted Whig leaders to name a suitable candidate for the rank of major, as well as three or four lieutenants). Scott was equally quick to take offense when the administration insisted that he move up his timetable for initiating the campaign against Mexico.

Democratic senator Thomas Hart Benton poisoned the atmosphere still further by authoring emergency legislation to create two additional major generals and four brigadier generals in the regular army, a blatantly partisan attempt to supersede long-serving Whig generals like Scott with loyal Democrats. The bill passed, although the Whigs in Congress did manage to reduce the number of new commissions to one major general and two brigadiers. In a letter to Secretary of War Marcy, Scott accused the administration of attempting to sabotage his efforts, complaining of "a fire upon my rear, from Washington, and the fire, in front, from the Mexicans."

Scott paid a high price for these indiscretions. Viewing the general's petulance as rank insubordination, Polk called a special cabinet meeting on May 25 to discuss the matter. The president and his advisers decided to relieve Scott of his role as field commander, denying him the opportunity to enhance his political fortunes on the battlefield. Secretary of War Marcy informed Scott that his services would no longer be required on the Rio Grande; instead, the general was to coordinate the war effort from his desk in Washington. Stunned by the severity of this punishment, Scott penned an extravagant apology, but Polk refused to reconsider his decision.

To replace Scott, Polk turned to Zachary Taylor, promoting him to the new major generalship that Benton's bill had created. Taylor's reputation had risen immeasurably following his victories at Palo Alto and Resaca de la Palma. By all outward appearances, Taylor could not have been more different from Winfield Scott. Gruff, disdainful of ceremony and military pomp, he preferred an old private's uniform and straw hat to the gold brocade of higher rank. But like his former superior, Taylor possessed a monumental ego that bruised easily. Sensitive to even the slightest criticism, Taylor would become churlish and uncooperative if he suspected that the administration did not fully appreciate his efforts.

When Polk declared war against Mexico, the United States was not ready to fight a war, much less to undertake a major campaign beyond its borders. The regular army consisted of less than 10,000 men, most of whom were scattered along the western frontier line in remote outposts—small units without experience in large-scale military operations. Under the direction of Secretary of War William Marcy, the government hastily transformed its provincial army into a fighting force capable of waging war on foreign soil. Construction began immediately on a fleet of steamboats to transport men and supplies to the theater of operations along the Rio Grande; in the interim the War Department purchased all the suitable vessels it could find. Arsenals, armories, and forges worked around the clock to provide the army with the sinews of war. At the Schuylkill Arsenal in Philadelphia, 4,000 men and women were employed making uniforms, shoes, and tents. Ironically, while Polk's commitment to territorial expansion stemmed in large part from his desire to preserve the Jeffersonian ideal of a simple, agrarian republic, the war now being waged to acquire new lands for the United States had instead quickened the pace of American industrial growth.

Mexico faced even more formidable problems as it mobilized for war. Unlike the United States, Spain's former colony lacked even a rudimentary industrial base, making it virtually impossible for the government to outfit an army at short notice. Years of corruption and neglect had left arsenals throughout the country either empty or stocked with notoriously unreliable firearms, obsolete since the Napoleonic Wars, which Mexico had purchased from Great Britain.

Moreover, the Mexican army reflected the political instability and deep racial divisions that had plagued the nation since independence. In recent years, it had virtually ceased to function as an instrument of national defense, dedicating itself almost exclusively to political intrigue. The officer class consisted largely of professional soldiers from Europe and Mexico's ruling elite. The rank and file was composed of irregularly paid and poorly fed peons, many of them Indians who spoke little or no Spanish. The government had for years resorted to impressment to staff its garrisons, but so high was the desertion rate that new recruits had to be taken from their villages chained in pairs. Aware of the shortcomings of its standing army, the Herrera regime in 1845 had tried to establish a national guard composed of patriotic volunteers, but its efforts had been nothing short of abysmal. In the nation's capital, 11 men had signed up on the first day of recruiting; in Puebla, only one volunteer had enlisted after two weeks.

By contrast, the declaration of war in the United States provoked a groundswell of martial enthusiasm. By some estimates more than 200,000 men responded to the Secretary of War's call for 50,000 volunteers. So many attempted to enlist in Tennessee that the selection had to be made by lottery. The quotas of some states were filled so quickly that young men moved to neighboring states to enlist.

Thousands of young American men raised on the epic historical novels of Sir Walter Scott eagerly volunteered, imagining themselves as knights errant on a glorious crusade. No doubt more than a few had also read William H. Prescott's *Conquest of Mexico,* published in 1843, a best-selling chronicle of the exploits of Spanish conquistador Hernan Cortés. Their dreams of similar adventures in a land that remained exotic and mysterious to Americans also contained unmistakably sexual undertones. Coexisting with the crude stereotypes of Mexicans in general was an exalted view of Mexican womanhood that fueled the heroic fantasies of American volunteers. Mexican women, many believed, were eager to be rescued from their degenerate mates by virile Anglo-Americans. As one popular song of the time, "They Wait for Us," suggested, U.S. soldiers could expect sexual conquests in Mexico as well as military ones:

> *The Spanish maid, with eye of fire,*
> *At balmy evenings turns her lyre*
> *And, looking to the Eastern sky,*
> *Awaits our Yankee chivalry*
> *Whose purer blood and valiant arms,*
> *Are fit to clasp her budding charms.*

Inevitably, the romance of warfare soon faded. In July, the volunteer regiments began arriving at Camargo, a bleak, windswept village on the San Juan River, a tributary of the Rio Grande, where Taylor had established his base of operations after the fall of Matamoros. The volunteer regiments' failure to take adequate sanitation precautions soon turned the camp into a quagmire of filth and disease, made all the more unbearable by blistering heat. During the next five weeks, 1,500 American troops, a staggering 12 percent of Taylor's force, died at Camargo of dysentery and other diseases.

While Taylor prepared to march south, American forces wasted little time in gaining control of Mexico's northernmost territories. In June, Colonel Stephen Watts Kearny marched his "Army of the West" from Fort Leavenworth, Kansas, along the Santa Fe Trail, seizing New Mexico without resistance in mid-August. Kearny then split his forces into three parts. Leaving a garrison behind to occupy New Mexico, Kearny placed Alexander Doniphan in command of an expedition to march south into Chihuahua, while he headed west across the Rocky Mountains with a contingent of 300 men to aid in the conquest of California. There, an expedition under the command of John C. Frémont had clashed with Mexican forces even before news of the outbreak of hostilities between the two countries arrived. U.S. Commodore John Sloat, acting on his instructions from Washington to seize Mexican ports along the Pacific in the event of war, captured Monterey on July 7 and San Francisco three days later. His successor as commander of the Pacific squadron, Commodore Robert Stockton, acting jointly with Frémont, declared California's annexation to the United States and organized a new territorial government, appointing himself governor.

Encouraged by the performance of its armies in the field, Washington continued to pursue diplomatic efforts to bring the conflict to a speedy conclusion. Polk and his cabinet remained convinced that Mexico lacked the will to fight, and on July 27, having learned of Taylor's success at Palo Alto and Resaca de la Palma, the administration sent a letter to the Mexican government offering to initiate peace negotiations. Having declined to discuss the crisis with Santa Anna earlier in the year, Polk now believed the time was ripe to open a dialogue with the deposed Mexican leader. Accordingly, Alexander Slidell Mackenzie, the brother of John Slidell, was dispatched to Havana to confer with the general, while the commodore of the Gulf fleet received instructions to allow Santa Anna to pass through the U.S. naval blockade of Veracruz should he attempt to do so.

In the summer of 1846, the president also returned to the idea of asking Congress for a special discretionary fund that could be used to facilitate negotiations with Mexican leaders. Since the administration had consistently maintained that it was not fighting a war of conquest against Mexico, it had as yet refrained from discussing publicly what territory it would demand as an indemnity if the United States won the war. Thus the so-called Two Million Dollar Bill referred only to the "adjustment of a boundary between the two Republics," although there was no doubt in Polk's mind that the money would be used as a down payment toward the purchase of California and New Mexico.

If the administration expected the Two Million Dollar Bill to pass easily, it had sorely misjudged the mood on Capitol Hill. Many congressmen on both sides of the aisle believed they had been stampeded into voting for a declaration of war, and now used the bill as an opportunity to renew the debate on the administration's war aims. Northern Whigs charged that the bill would enable the administration to acquire new lands for the extension of slavery. Taking up this theme, David Wilmot, a Pennsylvania Democrat, proposed an amendment to the Two Million Dollar Bill that would prohibit the institution in any territory acquired from Mexico. Professing no "morbid sympathy for the slave," Wilmot insisted that he sought only to "preserve . . . a fair country, a rich inheritance, where the sons of toil, of my own race and color, can live without the disgrace which association with negro slavery brings upon free labor." The Two Million Dollar Bill and the accompanying Wilmot Proviso passed the House by an 87 to 64 margin, but a southern filibuster prevented the bill from coming to a vote in the Senate before the session ended.

Wilmot's decision to confront the administration on the issue of slavery at this time appears to have been due to a range of concerns, of which the expansion of the "peculiar institution" into the West was only a part. A Van Buren Democrat, the Pennsylvania congressman continued to harbor the belief that the 1844 presidential nomination had been stolen from the party's rightful standard-bearer. Wilmot's partisan loyalties had also been sorely tested by Polk's patronage appointments in Pennsylvania, fears of political repercussions as a result of the Walker tariff—he had been the only congressman from the Keystone state to vote for the measure—and the administration's refusal to promote federally funded internal improvements. Like many Van Burenites, who tended to be ambivalent about the expansionist mania that gripped their party, Wilmot may also have been troubled by the administration's foreign policy agenda. While the All Oregon campaign pledge had not been an issue of great concern in the North in 1844, Polk's readiness to reach a compromise with Great Britain once in office had caused rumblings of discontent in that section of the country. The aggressiveness with which the administration had worked to obtain Texas, and its apparent determination to acquire additional territory in the Southwest at Mexico's expense, had given rise to feelings of betrayal among northern Democrats, reinforcing their suspicion that the president's priorities were southern ones.

The defeat of the Two Million Dollar Bill was a great disappointment to Polk. Convinced that slavery would never exist in New Mexico and California, the president failed to understand why the issue had been raised at all. "What connection slavery had with making peace with Mexico it is difficult to conceive," he noted with exasperation in his diary. Although its significance would not become fully apparent until later, the Wilmot Proviso introduced a new and ominous dimension to the debate over the war's aims. By raising anew the specter of slavery in the context of expansion, the Pennsylvania Democrat had driven a wedge between the free-soil and pro-slavery wings of the party, which in time would not only threaten Polk's territorial agenda but the very Union itself.

Still operating under the erroneous conviction that Mexican leaders would prefer to sell the United States the territory it demanded rather than prolong the war, Polk believed that by denying him the necessary funds, Congress had prevented him from making "an honorable peace" with

Mexico. It soon became evident, however, that the crisis could not be so easily or so quickly resolved, for the president had greatly underestimated the determination of Mexican leaders to resist American aggression; their stubborn defense of the nation's honor would remain undiminished even as hope for victory on the battlefield faded.

The highly volatile political situation in Mexico City also precluded the possibility of a quick negotiated settlement. In August General Paredes was arrested and deposed, his efforts to bring about the return of the Bourbon monarchy having alienated all but a handful of conservatives. A new interim government formed by General José Mariano Salas declined to consider Washington's July 27 peace overture and invited Santa Anna to return from exile. In mid-August the prodigal leader arrived in Veracruz, passing unmolested through the U.S. blockade of the port city. But instead of entering into peace negotiations with the Polk administration as he had promised, Santa Anna proceeded to organize an army with which to launch a counteroffensive against U.S. forces. Although it is unlikely that the American naval blockade could have prevented Santa Anna from returning in any case, the administration's secret diplomacy had failed utterly, having succeeded only in aiding the return of Mexico's most capable and energetic leader.

Characteristically, the administration reacted to Mexican intransigence by stiffening its resolve. If Mexico would not sue for peace, the United States was prepared to secure its objectives by force of arms. Having already received instructions to march on Monterrey, the largest city in northern Mexico, Taylor gathered the bulk of his army, some 6,000 men, and headed south, reaching the city on September 19. There he found the Mexican Army of the North, now under the command of Pedro Ampudia, dug in and prepared to defend the town.

It was Taylor's good fortune to be blessed throughout the war with some highly capable subordinates, one of whom was General William Worth, a former commandant of cadets at West Point. To Worth, Taylor assigned the task of leading 2,000 men on a flanking movement to the west, in order to cut off Ampudia's escape route. The battle began on September 21, with an ill-conceived frontal assault of the town by American forces. By the end of the day, Taylor's troops had been almost completely driven back with heavy losses; Worth, meanwhile, had gained steady ground against the Mexican hilltop fortifications that guarded the western approach to the city. The following day the noose around the city was tightened, and on the third day of fighting, U.S. and Mexican forces were battling for control of the streets of Monterrey.

On the morning of September 24, U.S. troops were preparing to renew their assault when Ampudia asked for a parley. Taylor initially demanded an unconditional surrender, but the American general was as anxious as his Mexican counterpart to avoid further fighting and quickly abandoned this uncompromising posture. With his army running low on ammunition, and discipline, after three days of hard fighting, beginning to break down, Taylor allowed Ampudia's force to evacuate the city, taking with it some of its arms and equipment. Since poor communications made it impossible for the two generals to obtain instructions from their respective capitals at short notice, Taylor and Ampudia signed an eight-week armistice, with the stipulation that the agreement could be rescinded later if either government found its terms unsatisfactory.

The United States was now in possession of northern Mexico, but for Polk the good news was offset by his irritation with Taylor who, he believed, should have accepted nothing less than the enemy's unconditional surrender. The president believed Taylor had missed a splendid opportunity to end the war by allowing the Mexican army to evacuate the city. "It was a great mistake," the president remarked when the news arrived in Washington. "It will only enable the Mexican army to reorganize and recruit so as to make another stand." Taylor's new orders from Washington pointedly refrained from congratulating the general on his victory and instructed him to terminate the armistice immediately.

The administration's unhappiness with the peace terms signed at Monterrey brought an immediate chill to relations between Polk and his commanding general in northern Mexico. Zachary Taylor was indignant when he learned of the administration's reaction and fired off a letter to Secretary of War William Marcy defending his conduct. In the months ahead the president would become increasingly irritated with his field commander, who expressed little enthusiasm for the administration's campaign strategy, but seemed deliberately noncommittal when asked to give his own opinions on how to prosecute the war.

The administration's displeasure with Taylor did not prevent the American people from hailing the first bona fide hero of the war. Not since Andrew Jackson's victory at New Orleans had the nation indulged in such hero worship. By late summer 1846, two biographies of the general were in print. Plays such as *The Siege of Monter[r]ey, or the Triumph of Rough and Ready,* were rushed into production within hours after the news of victory was received and performed to packed theaters in American cities.

The deteriorating relations between Polk and Taylor were aggravated by reports that the general's new-found fame had awakened in him a hunger for still greater rewards. Although Taylor had shown little interest in politics—he had never even voted in a presidential election—he was now being touted by the Whigs as a possible candidate in 1848. By year's end, Polk was complaining that Taylor "has been made giddy with the idea of the Presidency." Having sidelined one Whig general to keep him from making political capital of the war, Polk now found to his dismay that he had created another.

While the administration continued to hope for a decisive military victory, it also sought to undermine the authority of the Mexican government by other means. Well aware of the northern provinces' long history of resistance toward the centralist government in Mexico City, Washington instructed Taylor to establish good relations with the Mexican people and, wherever possible, to promote secessionist sentiment. American commanders were ordered to issue a proclamation stating that occupation forces had "come to overthrow the tyrants who have destroyed your liberties," and promising "to make no war upon the people of Mexico." To further win the support of those living in occupied territory, Taylor was ordered to pay for all supplies requisitioned by the invading army at fair market prices.

At Polk's request, Catholic priests were attached to the army to reassure Mexican citizens that their rights and religious customs would be protected. This policy did not sit well with some Protestants in the United States. In October a Presbyterian minister from Philadelphia called at the White House to request a chaplain's appointment in the army. Much to the president's annoyance, he used the occasion to make a number of intemperate remarks regarding the Catholic faith and criticized the administration for its decision to employ priests for duty in Mexico. "I have a great veneration and regard for Religion & sincere piety," Polk wrote in his diary that evening, "but a hypocrite or a bigotted [sic] fanatic without reason I cannot bear."

The administration's efforts to win the hearts and minds of the Mexican people stood little chance of success. Taylor showed no interest in establishing a dialogue with Mexican separatists, and even if he had, American racial attitudes proved to be an insurmountable barrier to friendly relations between the U.S. Army and the civilian population. An utter want of discipline among American troops, particularly among the volunteer regiments, also contributed to racial tensions, alienating federalists in northern Mexico who had long admired the American political system. According to George Gordon Meade, an officer in the regular army, the volunteers killed Mexican civilians "for no other object than their own amusement." The volunteers from Texas proved to be a particular problem, many having enlisted to avenge the deaths of friends or family members killed during the Revolution or the more recent border clashes between Texas and Mexico. "There has not been as much drunkenness and rioting here as at Matamoros," one soldier wrote from Monterrey, "but still several murders have been committed on both sides, mostly by Texans." Taylor admitted that "some disgraceful atrocities" had been committed by the Texas volunteers; on one occasion he had to personally reprimand a soldier who was found scalping his Mexican victims.

Having enlisted for 90-day terms, many Texans returned home shortly after the fall of Monterrey, but the depredations committed by American volunteers continued. After one of their men was found murdered, an Arkansas cavalry regiment massacred as many as 30 civilians who had sought safety in the mountains. Plundering proved to be a particularly serious problem. Taylor threatened to discharge soldiers caught with stolen property, but the practice quickly became so widespread that it was impossible to single out individuals for punishment. As a result, entire regiments were sent back to the rear, where they continued to harass the local population at Camargo.

Despite these breaches of discipline, the first six months of the war had been an astonishing success for the United States. The conquest of the Southwest had not been a bloodless one, nor was it yet complete. In both California and New Mexico, angry inhabitants would rise up against American occupying forces, which would not fully reassert their control over either territory until early the following year. Notwithstanding these setbacks, the administration's three-pronged campaign against Mexico had gone much as Polk had planned. And yet it had failed to achieve the desired result: a willingness on the part of the Mexican government to sue for peace.

While news of the triumph of American arms at Monterrey had been joyfully received in all quarters of the country, opposition to the war was growing. With increasing frequency, prominent Whigs were speaking out against the president's handling of the conflict, although they stopped short of questioning the country's right to wage war against Mexico. Daniel Webster and Henry Clay could both be counted among the president's detractors, but nonetheless proudly sent sons off to fight in the conflict. Neither would return. Clay's son would die in battle at Buena Vista; Webster's would succumb to typhoid fever after the peace treaty had been signed. Opposition to the war was strongest in New England, where the Whigs enjoyed a virtual monopoly of power in some states—Massachusetts voters would not send a Democrat to Congress during Polk's term of office. The region had long been a stronghold of antislavery groups, that now denounced the administration for deliberately provoking a war with Mexico to expand the "slave power."

Antiwar dissent was not confined to the political opposition. While Whigs were more willing for partisan reasons to voice their objections to the war, certain influential groups within the Democratic party were also troubled by the crisis and its possible consequences. John C. Calhoun, whose expansionist goals had been satisfied with Texas, remained staunchly opposed to the war, although this did not stop Van Burenites such as David Wilmot from suspecting that the party they had once served with such devotion was falling under the sway of southern interests. Nor was slavery the only concern. Now that the groundswell of jingoism had subsided, some sober-minded political leaders feared that the war would jeopardize the Oregon settlement, or even lead to a wider conflict involving Great Britain.

Nonetheless, the president could count on solid public support for the war effort, at least for the time being. With the exception of a handful of radical Whigs, most politicians of both parties who harbored doubts about the war were loath to say so publicly. But vocal dissent could be expected to rise if the war became a protracted one, and as the cost in human lives and material resources mounted. Polk himself expressed alarm at the spiraling costs of the war. Having anticipated a cheap and easy victory, the cost-conscious president had been shocked to learn in early November that the military budget for the coming fiscal year was $22 million above normal peacetime expenditures, a fact that the Whigs could be expected to use to their political advantage.

The results of the 1846 elections for the Thirtieth Congress brought more bad news for the administration. In 16 state contests in the North and Midwest, the Whigs picked up more than two dozen seats. While the war had not been an election issue, free-soil concerns that it was being waged primarily to enlarge the slave empire undoubtedly sapped Democratic voting strength in some northern states. The Whigs campaigned largely on traditional economic themes, skillfully capitalizing on voter concerns about the Walker Tariff and the Independent Treasury system. Local issues over which the administration had little if any control also played a part in the outcomes of various state elections, particularly in New York, where infighting between two rival factions had caused the Democrats to surrender 14 seats to the Whigs, as well as the governorship. Although the new crop of Whig congressmen would not take their seats until December 1847, the elections were a blunt reminder to the administration that its recent military successes did not translate into political gains at the ballot box.

Thus in the late fall of 1846, the president faced one of the most difficult decisions of his career. The United States could hold the territory it had already wrested from Mexican control and hope that its adversary would, at some point, come to the bargaining table. Since Mexican leaders had as yet shown no inclination to do so, this strategy required the administration to accept the likelihood of a long, drawn-out conflict. Such a prospect was hardly encouraging to an administration faced with an acrimonious sectional debate over the war's objectives, a shrinking Democratic majority in Congress, and less than enthusiastic support among party stalwarts.

A second option available to the administration was to escalate the war in order to bring it to a speedy conclusion. According to this school of thought, an aggressive campaign deep into Mexico's interior was needed to compel its leaders to accept defeat. "We are a go ahead people," argued Missouri senator Thomas Hart Benton, the principal advocate of an offensive strategy. Departing from his customary policy of seeking counsel from members of his cabinet, Polk in recent weeks had come to value Benton's advice on military matters, and throughout the month of November the Missourian was a frequent visitor at the White House.

On the other hand, an aggressive strategy involved a high degree of risk, and if unsuccessful could jeopardize everything U.S. forces had already accomplished. An invasion from the north was quickly ruled out as impractical for logistical reasons, for it would require U.S. troops to traverse hundreds of miles of arid and inhospitable terrain, leaving supply lines dangerously overextended and vulnerable to Mexican depredations. Another plan of attack involved seizing Veracruz, Mexico's largest port, but this proposal presented equally obvious drawbacks. Yellow fever wreaked havoc on the coastal population in the hottest months of the year, making a long-term U.S. occupation of the city impossible. If the administration decided to open a second front at Veracruz, it would, sooner or later, be forced either to withdraw its troops or order an assault on the capital, deep in the most densely populated region of Mexico. An American force would encounter notoriously poor mountain roads and inhospitable jungles eminently well suited to guerrilla warfare, conditions in which superior American artillery would be of little advantage. Moreover, up to this point U.S. forces had subdued only the most thinly populated regions of northern Mexico, far removed from the capital, where many years of opposition to the central government had weakened national allegiances. An invasionary force in the valley of Mexico could expect much stiffer resistance from the civilian population.

In view of the fact that American troops had, in the first six months of the war, already secured the administration's territorial objectives, an offensive strategy seemed perilous in the extreme. Any military reverses suffered by the United States would certainly delay rather than hasten negotiations with the Mexican government. Nonetheless, Polk never seemed to have doubted that U.S. arms would triumph. Anxious to get the war off dead center and growing increasingly frustrated with Mexican intransigence, the president agreed with Benton that an offensive strategy was the most expeditious way to conclude a peace on American terms. Secretary of State Buchanan, who with characteristic caution favored holding the Mexican territory in the north now controlled by U.S. forces, was slow to support the idea, but in the end the president's view prevailed. On November 17, 1846, with the unanimous agreement of his cabinet, Polk ordered that preparations be made to launch a seaborne invasionary force against Veracruz. The decision as to whether to proceed into the interior of Mexico would be made later, but the president had already made up his mind to authorize a march on the capital should Mexican leaders remain intractable.

The administration then turned to the matter of appointing a commander to head the campaign. General Taylor, Polk decided, was not the man for the job. Taylor had never been fully supportive of the plan to open a second front, and in any case Polk had no intention of giving him the opportunity to cover himself in more glory. Senator Benton suggested himself as a candidate for the job if the president would appoint him general-in-chief of the army. So great was the president's desire to have a stalwart Democrat in charge of military operations in Mexico that he actually considered the idea, but on further reflection decided that such a brazenly partisan maneuver would never be able to get the necessary congressional approval.

As the army's only other major general, Winfield Scott was the obvious choice for the Veracruz command. The president had not forgiven him for his partisan transgressions at the outset of the war and still doubted his loyalty to the administration. But the president could find no one else with sufficient stature and experience to conduct the campaign. Despite serious reservations, but convinced that "anybody would do better than Taylor," the president summoned Scott to the White House on November 19. In telling the general of his decision, Polk stated that he was now "willing that by-gones should be by-gones," and offered Scott command of the Veracruz invasion. Overcome with emotion, Scott "was so grateful & so much affected," the president recorded in his diary that evening, "that he almost shed tears."

CHAPTER

10

Conquering a Peace

Scott undertook his preparations for the Veracruz campaign with vigor and enthusiasm. Determined to avoid the pitfalls that had been his undoing when he had first been given overall command of the war effort back in May, Scott repeatedly expressed his unequivocal support of the administration's policies. The Whig general lavished praise on the president, declaring himself to be a bona fide "Polk-man." Remembering the administration's intolerance of delay, Scott left for the front a mere ten days after his meeting with Polk at the White House. He arrived at Camargo on January 3, 1847, and promptly ordered Taylor to send 9,000 troops back to the Rio Grande in preparation for the invasion of Veracruz.

The cooperative spirit with which Scott approached his new command was destined to be short-lived. Believing that he now enjoyed the president's full confidence, Scott was shocked when he learned soon after his meeting at the White House that Thomas Hart Benton had been Polk's initial choice for the assignment, and suspected that the administration might still try to supersede him. Relations between the two men were further soured by an incident involving Scott's decision to court martial a colonel with strong ties to the Democratic party. Assuming that Scott's motives were entirely political, the president reprimanded his general-in-chief and reinstated the officer. By the time the Veracruz invasion had been launched, the honeymoon between Polk and General Scott was over.

Scott was not the only Whig general who felt unappreciated by the administration. Zachary Taylor was furious when he received Scott's orders to give up the bulk of his force for the Veracruz campaign and assume a defensive position in northern Mexico. Fearing that his star was about to be eclipsed, he dashed off a stinging message to Scott, professing to be "personally mortified and outraged" by the new strategy. When Washington suggested that it would be unwise for Taylor to go beyond Monterrey, the general in a fit of pique sent a force to occupy Saltillo, 50 miles to the southwest. Refusing to be relegated to the secondary role now assigned to him, Taylor would not abandon his advanced position even when Scott explicitly ordered him to do so. The president fumed: "It is manifest that Gen'l Taylor is wholly incompetent for so large a command."

Though frustrated by his inability to control the activities of his generals in the field, Polk took it on himself to supervise every aspect of the war effort, subjecting all decisions made at the War Department to the closest scrutiny. Always mindful of government inefficiency, the president insisted on being kept constantly informed by Secretary Marcy of military expenditures. Much to his astonishment, Polk discovered that the Quartermaster's Department had ordered thousands of wagons for the campaigns in Mexico, despite the fact that pack mules were better suited to Mexico's rugged terrain. The president was also annoyed to find that the army was purchasing horses and mules in the United States and transporting them to the theater of operations, when such animals were readily available at a fraction of the cost in Mexico.

In the new session of Congress, which had opened in December, the grumbling over Polk's war aims continued.

The president pushed once again for a bill to facilitate negotiations with Mexico, this time for $3 million, and legislation to create an additional ten regiments in the regular army. Both bills passed, but not before a coalition of northern Democrats and Whigs in the House made another unsuccessful attempt to resurrect the Wilmot Proviso. This in turn elicited vigorous protests from John C. Calhoun, who accused northern politicians of using the war to attack the institution of slavery. Though angered by the conduct of both sides, Polk was particularly upset by Calhoun's constant criticism of the administration's war policies. Having worked hard for the annexation of Texas and tariff reduction—two issues of paramount concern to Calhoun— the president expected greater loyalty from the South Carolina senator. "He is wholly selfish, & I am satisfied has no patriotism," Polk grumbled.

While American civilian and military leaders squabbled, Mexico hovered on the brink of anarchic dissolution. The presence of foreign armies on its soil had failed to unite its people, but rather had revived long-standing animosities, particularly among the privileged classes. Desperate for funds to pay for the war, the Mexican government tried to obtain forced loans from the Catholic Church, sparking a heated confrontation between ecclesiastical leaders and Mexican federalists who had long resented the Church's wealth and power.

Santa Anna, meanwhile, having learned that an invasion of Veracruz was imminent, resolved to move immediately against General Taylor's army, the weaker of the two American forces. The Mexican leader hastily assembled an army composed of conscripts and the remnants of Ampudia's forces at San Luis Potosí and headed north, a grueling march over desolate terrain made all the more difficult by bitterly cold weather. Some 3,000 troops deserted along the way, leaving Santa Anna with an army of 17,000.

Once again, the Mexican army's formidable troop strength was no indication of its combat readiness, its numerical advantage counting for little against Taylor's well-fed, well-armed, and well-supplied forces.

On February 23, 1847, Santa Anna threw his bedraggled troops against a carefully chosen American defensive position at Buena Vista, six miles south of Saltillo. Twice the Mexican infantry came close to turning Taylor's left flank, but with victory in their grasp were thrown back, owing to the timely arrival of American reinforcements from Saltillo and superior American firepower. In the afternoon, Santa Anna ordered a massed assault against the center of the American line, where Taylor had concentrated his artillery. Again Mexican troops almost succeeded in driving the Americans from the field, but were finally repulsed by withering cannon fire.

Anticipating another attack the following day, Taylor was astonished to find the Mexican army gone the next morning. His supplies exhausted and his troops hungry, Santa Anna had given the order to withdraw, and his army was now lumbering back down the road to San Luis Potosí. Both generals claimed victory, but in fact little had been gained by either side. Although Taylor's Army of Occupation remained in control of northern Mexico, Santa Anna had come very close to reversing Mexico's fortunes on the battlefield. Taylor wisely declined to pursue the retreating Mexican army and withdrew to Monterrey, having fought his last battle of the war.

As Santa Anna made his way southward, news reached him of a revolt in Mexico City. Recent anticlerical legislation authorizing the confiscation and sale of church property passed by the federalists had divided the capital into warring camps. His political stock on the rise again after Buena Vista, Santa Anna was urged by both groups to put an end to the crisis. The Mexican leader promptly hammered out a compromise with the Church, which agreed to a hefty contribution to the war effort in exchange for the repeal of the anticlerical legislation. With this much-needed infusion of cash and some semblance of order in the capital now restored, Santa Anna set out to raise yet another force to meet Scott's army.

On March 9, 8,600 U.S. troops landed unopposed near Veracruz. After capturing the fortress at the mouth of the harbor, Scott began shelling the city on March 22, a bombardment that would continue for the next 88 hours. Once in control of Veracruz, Scott wasted little time moving inland, away from the dreaded yellow fever that plagued the coastal plain. By April his army was on the march, along the road leading into the country's mountainous midsection toward the capital.

News of the fall of Veracruz and the Battle of Buena Vista reached Washington in early April. To Polk it now seemed only a matter of time before Mexico bowed to the inevitable and sued for peace. Accordingly, the cabinet decided to send to Mexico a peace commissioner, who would travel with General Scott's army and have the authority to negotiate a treaty when the Mexican government signaled a willingness to do so. Polk and his advisers decided to give this important assignment to Nicholas Trist, the chief clerk of the State Department. Fluent in Spanish, Trist came highly recommended by James Buchanan, who frequently left him in charge of the State Department when he was away from Washington. Perhaps equally attractive from the president's point of view, Trist's Democratic credentials were impeccable; married to a granddaughter of Thomas Jefferson, Trist could presumably be counted on to serve the administration faithfully.

After some discussion over the conditions the United States would be willing to accept from Mexico, the cabinet instructed Trist to demand the cession of New Mexico and Upper California and secure the Rio Grande as the southern boundary of Texas. If possible, Trist was also authorized to negotiate for the acquisition of Lower California and the right of passage for American citizens across the Tehuantepec isthmus. For this Polk was prepared to pay $30 million, a modest price, he believed, given the inestimable value of the land and the fact that it would cost the United States much more if the war dragged on.

But once again, Polk's belief that an end to the war was in sight proved unwarranted. At Cerro Gordo, a mountain pass midway between Veracruz and the capital, Santa Anna was preparing to halt the American advance. The Mexican general had chosen his position carefully, concentrating his forces along the main road to take advantage of the steep hills on either side. But Santa Anna had not counted on Scott's West Point-trained army engineers who, after a thorough reconnaissance of the area, cut a path through the mountains, enabling Scott to throw troops and artillery against a weakly defended left flank. By the time Santa Anna realized that the primary American assault would not come from the main road, it was too late to redeploy his forces. On April 17, U.S. troops seized one of the outlying foothills on the Mexican left and the following morning stormed Telegraph Hill, the linchpin of the Mexican defensive line. The battle soon turned into a rout as Mexican troops broke rank and fled in disorder. The way to Mexico City now lay open to Winfield Scott and his triumphant army.

With the remnants of the Mexican army in full retreat, the war seemed to be over, but Scott's drive to the capital suddenly and unexpectedly stalled. The war legislation under which the American volunteers had enlisted required them to serve 12 months or the duration of the conflict. After almost 11 months of service, many had had their fill of war and were anxious to go home. Unable to persuade his battle-weary troops to extend their terms of enlistment and serve until the war's end, Scott decided to allow the volunteer regiments to withdraw immediately. During the first week in May, some 3,000 soldiers marched back the way they had come, down the national highway to Veracruz.

Frustrated by his inability to march on the capital and end the war, Scott may have felt that the glory and honor he had hoped to achieve by the campaign were slipping from his grasp. In any case, when the general-in-chief learned that Polk had appointed Nicholas Trist to negotiate a treaty with Mexico, he sensed another threat by the administration to undercut his authority. Arriving in Veracruz on May 6, the American diplomat sent a sealed dispatch from Buchanan to the Mexican government to Scott's headquarters in Jalapa, which he asked the U.S. commander to forward to the capital. Incredibly, Scott refused, indignant at being asked to serve as a messenger for a mere State Department clerk, and returned the sealed dispatch to Trist. When the American diplomat arrived at Jalapa, the two men exchanged angry letters, refusing even to meet with each other, a situation that continued for several weeks. Scott asked to be relieved of command, a request the president, who was appalled by his general's "folly and ridiculous vanity," no doubt would have granted had not the military campaign entered such a critical phase. Scott and Trist eventually patched up their quarrel, but the rupture between Polk and his general-in-chief was now irreparable.

The summer months of 1847 were a time of inactivity for both sides. In mid-May Scott moved his army to Puebla, 75 miles east of Mexico City, to await reinforcements. For the next ten weeks, the army fought boredom and disease while Mexican guerrillas harassed his supply trains coming up from Veracruz. Fortunately for Scott,

Mexico's political leaders were unable to take advantage of his vulnerable position, being more deeply divided in the wake of the disaster at Cerro Gordo than ever before. A bellicose war faction remained unbowed, predicting that the invaders would be crushed if they dared to attack the capital. Many liberal federalists were considerably more circumspect, and had come to the conclusion that some form of negotiated settlement with the United States was necessary. Some even hoped for an American victory, which would discredit the Mexican army and destroy its political influence. No faction, however, was willing to assume responsibility for initiating peace talks. The Mexican Congress was so paralyzed by dissension that angry delegates frequently boycotted the sessions, making it impossible for the government to deal with the crisis for lack of a quorum. Thus Santa Anna remained in power, a dictator by default.

Polk spent the latter part of June and early July on a tour of the northeastern states, one of his few trips away from the nation's capital during his four years in office. The trip was not intended to shore up public support for the war effort, since most of the congressional elections in the states on his itinerary had already been held. Nonetheless, the excursion was a risky undertaking for the chief executive, who would be venturing into the very heart of the region most opposed to his wartime policies. On June 22 the president and a small entourage set out by rail for Baltimore, and in the days ahead traveled slowly northward, making stops at towns and cities along the route, including Philadelphia, New York, Boston, and Portland. The reception the president encountered was overwhelmingly enthusiastic, with public dignitaries of both parties and thousands of citizens turning out to greet him. Well pleased with the tour, Polk wrote to Sarah as his journey was nearing its close: "Nothing of a party or of an unpleasant character occurred anywhere." For the president the trip helped to reinforce his belief that a common purpose bound all citizens of the republic, regardless of party or regional loyalties, a conviction that had been sorely tested in recent months. Mindful of the disturbing divisions the war had caused, Polk stressed the need for national harmony at each public appearance. In Augusta, Maine, the president observed: "We live in different latitudes—we are engaged in different pursuits—and it is natural that we should entertain different sentiments on questions of a local or sectional character; but we are still brethren."

In Mexico, meanwhile, Santa Anna seemed uncertain whether to negotiate with the Americans or succumb to the blandishments of the war party. The Mexican general regrouped his forces and prepared to defend the capital, while simultaneously sending out peace feelers through intermediaries to the American camp. These overtures failed to yield productive results, and on August 7, Scott's army, now strengthened and numbering some 14,000 men, marched out of Puebla toward the capital. One week later the army descended into the Valley of Mexico, where Scott and his engineers paused to take stock of the situation. Choosing two southern approaches to the city in an effort to bypass Santa Anna's outer defenses, Scott launched an assault on August 19; the next day, after fierce fighting at two suburbs, Contreras and Churubusco, the Mexican army was forced to abandon its positions and fall back to the interior lines it had constructed at the causeways leading into the city.

Here on the outskirts of the capital Scott halted his attack. The American general had no desire to seize Mexico City by force, having suffered more than a thousand casualties in the recent fighting. A drive into the capital would only create panic and disorder, dispersing the government and causing the peace process further delays. Receiving information that the Mexican government was at last ready to negotiate, Scott proposed an armistice to discuss peace terms. The beleaguered Santa Anna, now desperate and stalling for time, gladly accepted.

The truce held for two weeks, allowing Nicholas Trist to meet on several occasions with a delegation of Mexican peace commissioners. Though the Santa Anna government, torn by peace and war factions, appeared reluctant to give ground on any issue, a constructive dialogue was quickly established between Trist and his Mexican counterparts. After considerable wrangling, Trist abandoned Polk's demand for Lower California, while the Mexican commissioners agreed to cede Upper California and New Mexico for $30 million. On the American demand for a Rio Grande boundary, however, the peace commissioners stood firm, insisting on Mexican control of the trans-Nueces region. Though Trist was doubtful that Polk would accept such a proposal, he considered the terms a partial victory, having secured the Mexican government's compliance with the president's other demands. Accordingly, he agreed to forward the proposal on to Washington.

Before Trist could do so, Santa Anna, apparently yielding to pressure from the war party, ordered his commissioners back to the negotiating table with new conditions that seemed calculated to put an end to talk of peace altogether. Ignoring the fact that an American army sat just outside the capital, the Mexican delegates now refused to cede New Mexico, and agreed to give up only a small portion of northern California. Trist, realizing that these terms would be wholly unacceptable to his government, broke off negotiations. Scott now prepared to resume hostilities.

The delay proved to be a costly one for American forces, for Santa Anna had used the armistice to shore up his defenses in the capital, a direct violation of the agreement. On September 8, Scott ordered an assault on Molino del Rey, an iron foundry on the southwestern edge of the capital, which was taken after heavy fighting. Four days later U.S. troops stormed Chapultepec castle, and on September 13 Scott's troops seized control of two causeways leading into the city.

Santa Anna, realizing that the capital could no longer be defended, evacuated his army that night. Scott's forces entered Mexico City on September 14, where they were greeted by public demonstrations and sporadic violence. Angry mobs resisted the American occupation for the next two days, prompting Scott to declare martial law. On September 15 Santa Anna resigned the presidency, although he continued to fight on as head of the army, still hoping for a victory—or at least the appearance of one—that would rally the nation behind him once again.

As yet unaware of these dramatic developments, and despite the enthusiastic reception accorded Polk on his tour of the Northeast, Americans by the fall of 1847 viewed the war with growing frustration. The Whigs had won a majority in the House of Representatives and could be expected to obstruct the administration's war policies when the Thirtieth Congress convened in December. In New England, "Conscience Whigs" condemned the conflict as an immoral conspiracy to extend the slave empire, a sentiment echoed with increasing conviction by northern Democrats, who were now rallying behind the Wilmot Proviso in an effort to prohibit slavery in any of the lands seized from Mexico. Fearful of the war's impact on party unity, statesmen of both parties called for the government to formally disavow any interest in acquiring Mexican territory. Even supporters of the war had broken rank with the administration. Thomas Hart Benton had ceased to advise Polk on military affairs, angered by the War Department's decision to court-martial his son-in-law John C. Frémont, who had refused to obey an order to give up the governorship of California to Stephen Watts Kearny.

While those who criticized Polk's war policies were motivated by a variety of reasons, sympathy for Mexico was not one of them. Indeed, many administration critics, fearing that the war would result in the incorporation of a sizable nonwhite population unfit for republican institutions, employed a brand of racist rhetoric similar to that of the most determined expansionists. Ohio senator Thomas Corwin described the Mexican people as a "half-savage, half-civilized race," in one of the more scathing anti-administration speeches delivered during the course of the war. Unitarian minister Theodore Parker, perhaps the country's most eloquent and impassioned advocate for peace, viewed Mexicans as "a wretched people; wretched in their origin, history and character," a race destined, regardless of American policies, to "melt away as the Indians before the white man."

But while the opponents of the war grew more vocal, public support for seizing even more territory from Mexico than Polk or his advisers had initially envisioned was rapidly gaining ground. In the fall of 1847, the expansionist press began to call not merely for the acquisition of Mexico's northernmost provinces, but for further cessions below the Rio Grande, while some demanded nothing less than that country's complete absorption by the United States. The demands for annexing all or at the very least a major portion of Mexico received the support of some of the most celebrated heroes of the war. On their return to the United States, General William Worth, General John Quitman, Commodore Robert Stockton, and others argued for some form of continued American military presence in Mexico after the war was over.

The call for the annexation of Mexico was not new; a year before the war began, the *Democratic Review* predicted its absorption by the United States "at some future period," while most Americans believed that the Mexican people would eventually fade before the inexorable march of "the unthralled Saxon." Few gave the idea much serious consideration, however, focusing instead on territorial objectives that seemed both readily attainable and relevant to national interests. But with the conquest of Mexico in 1847, the issue of that country's future was suddenly thrust to the forefront of the expansion debate. The collapse of political authority in Mexico, expansionists argued, freed American policy makers from any obligations to respect that country's sovereignty. Having not only been defeated on the battlefield but utterly vanquished, Mexico had lost its right to self-determination; whether it continued to exist as a nation at all was a matter for the United States to decide.

Much like the issues that had fueled the American thrust to the Pacific, the arguments employed in defense of the "All Mexico" movement spoke to a wide array of goals and concerns. In part, the idea was merely a consequence of the rampant national chauvinism that had fired the imagination of Americans throughout the decade, the victories in Mexico having given rise to ever more grandiose imperial ambitions. Mexico's vast silver reserves and tremendous agricultural potential were clearly paramount in the minds of some advocates for absorption. Railroad promoters, now assured of American control of the Pacific but daunted by the prospect of having to straddle the Rocky Mountains to get there, saw that Mexico offered a number of more accessible transcontinental routes. Others argued that the mounting costs of the war required the United States to demand a much larger territorial indemnity from Mexico.

As in earlier phases of Manifest Destiny, the threat of European meddling in the western hemisphere—and the intrigues of the British, in particular—proved to be among the most compelling arguments on behalf of annexation. General Mariano Paredes' brief flirtation with Spanish monarchists—a move that appeared to have the covert sanction of the British government—enabled expansionists to argue that its weak neighbor was vulnerable to European intrigue and thus imperiled American hemispheric interests. Mexican instability, of course, was due in no small measure to the United States, which had seized vast portions of Mexico's domain, blockaded its harbors, defeated its armies, toppled its government, and occupied its capital. But this did not deter American expansionists from pointing with alarm to Mexico's collapse, and declaring, without the least trace of irony, that its prostrate condition necessitated annexation by the United States to save it from European interference!

Because the annexation of Mexico, unlike earlier Manifest Destiny objectives, would necessarily involve the incorporation of a large, alien population, expansionists emphasized the American mission to "extend the area of freedom" more than ever before. The United States had a moral obligation, they argued, to instruct its Latin American neighbors in the lessons of civic virtue and self-government. "I would with a magnanimous and kindly hand gather these wretched people within the fold of republicanism," Commodore Stockton declared at a dinner held in his honor. The task of regenerating Mexico should go forward whether its people approved it or not, for any resistance to such a noble effort, expansionists insisted, would in time give way to enlightenment and gratitude. As the New York *Herald* declared, "Like the Sabine virgins, she will soon learn to love her ravisher."

Be that as it may, many Anglo-Americans balked at the prospect of assimilating a people whom they held in utter contempt. Undaunted, expansionists offered a number of plans for annexation, many of which were designed to allay these racial anxieties. Senator Ambrose H. Sevier, chairman of the Foreign Relations committee, proposed that the U.S. Army occupy the country and extend naturalization laws to Castilian Spaniards, while confining the darker-skinned segments of the population, *mestizos* and Indians, to tribal lands similar to those allocated to the indigenous peoples of the United States. The *Democratic Review* suggested that American soldiers be encouraged to remain in Mexico when the war ended, creating a basis for Anglo-Saxon acculturation. On another occasion it proposed that the United States establish some form of colonial rule in Mexico until its people could be properly instructed in the ways of self-government. Even a few Whig newspapers, unable to resist this tempting new entree on the expansionist menu, weighed in with their own suggestions of how the absorption of Mexico could best be accomplished. The *National Whig,* a journal founded to promote Zachary Taylor's presidential bid, proposed that the provinces of Mexico should be encouraged to draft new state constitutions based on republican principles; they could then be admitted to the Union on an individual basis.

Though public support for the All Mexico movement was undoubtedly on the rise in the fall of 1847, reaching across sectional and, to a much lesser extent, partisan lines, many politicians were not yet ready to endorse the new expansionist agenda until they could be certain of its popularity at the grassroots level. One indicator of the movement's growing strength was the conversion of James Buchanan. Having asked Polk to publicly forswear all territorial demands when the war began, Buchanan could now be found among the most strenuous champions of American imperialism, a position that he no doubt hoped would stand him in good stead with expansionist Democrats when the party chose a presidential nominee the following spring. The secretary of state's blatant efforts to position himself for the 1848 election greatly annoyed the president, who had not forgotten that Buchanan had experienced a similar about-face on the Oregon question.

Polk's principal concern as the war drew to a close was not the acquisition of more territory but the need to conclude a peace before the next session of Congress. The two issues were closely linked, however, for Polk was now convinced that the only way to bring about a settlement with Mexico was to send a clear and unequivocal message to its leaders that they could expect increasingly punitive peace terms from the United States the longer they held out. Thus during the first week in September, unaware that Scott's army was encamped at the gates of Mexico City, Polk and the cabinet began to consider ways in which Trist's April instructions might be modified. All agreed with the president that the United States should reduce its offer for New Mexico and the Californias from $30 million to $15 million. In addition, some members of the cabinet believed that the United States should now demand a larger territorial indemnity from Mexico, one which would include Tampico, Mexico's second largest port. In the end, rather than confuse matters by sending Trist new instructions, Polk and his advisers agreed to wait until more news from Mexico City arrived before instructing the diplomat to take a harder line.

In early October, Polk received unofficial word that Trist's negotiations with Mexican peace commissioners had broken down. Incensed by Mexican "obstinacy," the president was now convinced that the Santa Anna government had entered into peace talks merely as a ploy to gain time. Believing that any further contact between Trist and Mexican negotiators would create the impression that the United States was anxious to conclude a treaty under any terms, Polk ordered Buchanan to recall his diplomat; any future peace overtures would now have to be initiated by the government of Mexico. To increase the pressure on its leaders to come to terms, the president decided that henceforth the costs of the war would be borne by the

Mexican people. American armies in Mexico, which had formerly paid for all goods and services in an effort to win the support of the local populace, were now instructed to levy forced requisitions for such goods as they required.

Once Polk learned the full details of Trist's discussions with the Mexican government, which had refused to cede New Mexico and insisted on the trans-Nueces as a buffer zone as a condition for peace, his confidence in the diplomatic representative vanished. "Mr Trist has managed the negotiation very bunglingly and with no ability," the president declared. "I thought he had more sagacity and common sense than to make the propositions he has made."

On October 8, two days after Polk issued the order recalling Trist, organized resistance to the American invasion came to an end. After the fall of the nation's capital Santa Anna had marched to Puebla, where he made a rather half-hearted attempt to dislodge the American garrison. When that failed, he moved his troops in the first week of October against U.S. reinforcements coming up the road from Veracruz. The discouraged remnants of the Mexican army were quickly driven back at Huamantla. When a popular American officer was cut down by sniper fire, his enraged troops sacked the town, committing "every species of outrage," one soldier wrote in a letter to his family. "Old women and girls were stripped of their clothing. . . . Men were shot by dozens while concealing their property . . . while drunken soldiers, yelling and screeching, were breaking open houses or chasing some poor Mexicans who had abandoned their houses and fled for life. Such a scene I never hope to see again. It . . . made [me] for the first time, ashamed of my country."

Shortly thereafter Santa Anna was relieved of command and later sent into exile (the redoubtable leader's talent for political intrigue remained undiminished, however, and he would return to power five years later). The collapse of the war party brought a measure of stability to the Mexican political scene. In the wake of Santa Anna's fall, a coalition of moderates established an interim government and emerged as the dominant faction when the Mexican Congress convened in late October. This did not mean, however, that a clear and consistent peace policy on the part of the Mexican government was quick to emerge. Some representatives called for the complete evacuation of American troops before negotiations with the United States could begin, a demand Polk would not possibly consider. A group of radical federalists, or *puros*, meanwhile, continued to regard the Church and the army as a greater danger to the country than Scott's forces and favored a prolonged U.S. military occupation. Some *puros* even advocated protectorate status for Mexico, thus echoing the sentiments of American ultraexpansionists.

Uncertain though the political situation remained, the prospects for peace had improved considerably by the time Trist received his recall notice on November 16. Trist thought Polk's decision to suspend negotiations was a mistake; nonetheless, he had every intention of obeying his instructions and informed Buchanan that he hoped to leave within ten days. It would take longer for the army to provide him with an escort to Veracruz, however, and while he waited, the American diplomat came under considerable pressure from several quarters to take advantage of the new government's willingness to reach an accord with the United States. The interim Mexican president, the British minister, even General Scott—who had settled his quarrel with Trist and was now on the closest of terms with him—urged the American envoy to remain in Mexico and complete his diplomatic errand. Flattered by these expressions of confidence in his abilities, Trist came to the conclusion that the opportunity for peace could not be allowed to pass. Hoping to persuade his superiors in Washington of the wisdom of such a course, Trist composed a letter more than 60 pages long explaining his decision to disregard his recall notice and enter into negotiations with the new government.

Meanwhile, with the All Mexico movement continuing to gather steam, and the war's opponents calling for a peace that would leave Mexico with its pre-war boundaries intact, Polk was coming under increasing pressure to spell out the administration's territorial goals. In his annual message to Congress delivered on December 7, 1847, the president for the first time stated publicly what he had said privately all along: that Upper California and New Mexico would not be returned to Mexico, but rather would be taken by the United States to cover the costs of the war. Polk rejected out of hand his critics' call for a peace without territorial compensation. "The doctrine of no territory is the doctrine of no indemnity," the president declared, "and if sanctioned, would be a public acknowledgement that our country was wrong . . . an admission unfounded in fact, and degrading to the national character." While Polk refused to commit himself on the subject of Mexican annexation, he did not rule out the idea, either; he had long since lost patience with Mexican leaders and favored increasing the size of the territorial indemnity the longer the war dragged on. Polk declined to state what the administration might do if the Mexican government continued to delay peace talks, but he left no doubt that it could expect serious repercussions if the crisis remained unresolved. Unless an agreement with Mexico was reached soon, Polk noted ambiguously, the United States would have no choice but to "continue to occupy her country with our troops, taking the full measure of indemnity into our own hands, and must enforce the terms which our honor demands."

During the regular Saturday cabinet meeting at the White House on January 15, Trist's dispatch arrived for

Secretary Buchanan. If the American envoy had hoped that the administration would approve of his decision to continue negotiations, he was sorely mistaken. Whereas Trist had come to see himself as a freewheeling envoy without portfolio acting on his own initiative, the president regarded his diplomat in Mexico as a government functionary whose only job was to do as he was told. To Polk, a loyal Democrat who had never questioned nor hesitated to obey the dictates of party leaders, Trist's deliberate act of defiance was incomprehensible. "I have never in my life felt so indignant," Polk sputtered after reading Trist's long-winded defense of his actions. "He has acted worse than any man in the public employ whom I have ever known."

The president's ire was compounded by the fact that Trist's new-found admiration of General Scott had led him to take Scott's side in yet another partisan squabble involving the general and Democrats under his command. In November Scott had ordered the arrest of a trio of Democratic generals, one of whom was Polk's old friend Gideon Pillow, for publicly criticizing his conduct of the campaign. The affair was the last straw for Polk, who had already made the decision to recall Scott when Trist's letter arrived. Ever inclined to believe the worst of others, Polk concluded that Scott and Trist were collaborating against him. Trist "has become the tool of Gen'l Scott and his menial instrument," the president declared. By the end of the month his anger had not subsided, and Polk ordered Major General William O. Butler, Scott's successor as general-in-chief, to remove his insubordinate diplomat from headquarters and to inform the Mexican authorities that Trist had no diplomatic powers to draft a treaty.

In Mexico City, Trist was anxiously trying to hammer out an agreement before these new orders arrived. Despite the need for urgency, the negotiations proceeded with painful slowness, and with no agreement in sight by the end of January, it appeared as if a treaty would not be concluded in time. Frustrated, Trist declared the negotiations at an end. The ultimatum proved to be the breakthrough the American diplomat needed. Realizing that they could not expect more favorable terms from another administration representative, the Mexican peace delegation asked Trist to return to the bargaining table and accepted the American demands without further objections.

On February 2, 1848, Nicholas Trist and Mexican peace commissioners signed the Treaty of Guadalupe Hidalgo on the outskirts of Mexico City. In the principal articles of the treaty, Mexico ceded Upper California and New Mexico to the United States and agreed to recognize the Rio Grande as the boundary of Texas. In return, Mexico received $15 million, as well as the assumption by the United States of $3 million in unpaid American claims against the Mexican government.

A copy of the treaty arrived in Washington on February 19. Upset though he was by Trist's conduct, the president could see that the terms of the agreement gave the administration everything it had asked for, and at the price it was willing to pay. Polk called a special Sunday cabinet meeting to discuss whether the treaty should be sent to the Senate. Buchanan and Walker, who now saw eye to eye on matters of expansion, both favored rejection of the treaty on the grounds that it did not give the United States a large enough territorial indemnity. Polk himself believed that the United States was entitled to a larger chunk of Mexico's domain, but he was also aware of the risks should the administration reject Trist's handiwork. To demand that Mexico cede additional territory would almost certainly mean further hostilities, and Polk could not rely on the Whig-controlled House to continue to vote for military appropriations. Even if the United States managed to obtain a treaty granting a larger territorial cession, it was by no means certain that the Senate would ratify such an agreement. In any case, it was imperative that an agreement of some kind be reached soon, for if the Whigs managed to capture the White House in November, there existed the very real possibility that Washington would abandon its demands for any territorial concession from Mexico whatsoever. Believing that the proposed treaty offered the best option available to him, Polk decided to send the document to the Senate.

By this time, however, the country was so divided over the goals of the war that considerable doubt remained as to whether a treaty involving even a limited cession from Mexico could muster the two-thirds majority in the Senate. For two weeks of debate the fate of the treaty hung in the balance, with some senators denouncing the agreement for not taking enough territory from Mexico, while others were equally opposed because it took too much. Resistance to the treaty was strong in the Foreign Relations Committee, some of whose members favored sending an entirely new commission to negotiate a peace with Mexico. But in the end, many senators on both sides of the territorial issue seem to have come to the conclusion that the terms of the treaty, however unpalatable, were far preferable to the unknown consequences of rejection. The Senate ratified the treaty on March 10 by a vote of 38 to 14, with four abstentions.

Now that the war was over, the All Mexico movement faded even more quickly than it had emerged, as did the need to regenerate the Mexican people. Spurning the opportunity to appropriate lands occupied by millions of non-whites, Anglo-Americans seemed to want peace more than they wanted Mexico. Ironically, the racism that had helped to fuel Manifest Destiny also defined its limits. The jingoistic New York *Herald* conceded after the Senate voted to ratify the treaty: "perhaps it is better that we should swallow that country by separate mouthfuls, for fear it might injure our digestive organs . . . ."

The incessant feuding among the principal actors of the American war effort continued long after hostilities ended. The president could not bring himself to forgive Trist, unable to admit that his errant envoy's disobedience had spared him enormous political problems by successfully terminating an unpopular and divisive war. The American diplomat, he raged, "has proved himself to be an impudent and unqualified scoundrel." Ordered by Polk to leave Mexico, Trist refused, insisting that he was now a private citizen and could go where he pleased. General Butler had him arrested and expelled from the country. As a final indignity, the government refused to pay Trist's salary while he was negotiating the Treaty of Guadalupe Hidalgo, covering his expenses only up to the time his recall notice arrived in Mexico City. General Scott, the most distinguished general the United States produced in the period between the Revolution and the Civil War, received even rougher treatment at the hands of the Polk administration. In the spring of 1848, Scott was ordered to stand before a court of inquiry to investigate the charges he and his Democratic accusers had made against each other. The old soldier weathered the controversy, although it probably cost him the 1848 Whig presidential nomination, which went to another enemy of the administration, Zachary Taylor.

The fault for these squabbles was by no means Polk's alone. His critics were self-important and exceedingly temperamental men, who would have taxed the forbearance of even the most patient commander-in-chief. At the same time, however, the president's need to be in total control of every situation led inevitably to friction with his subordinates. Polk's hands-on style of management worked well enough in Washington, where a small bureaucracy discharged its duties under the watchful eye of the chief executive. But it had been impossible for the administration to supervise the operations of American troops on foreign soil with similar exactitude or such close attention to detail. Far removed from the seat of government, American military leaders and diplomatic agents enjoyed a freedom of action that Polk found enormously frustrating. In an atmosphere already poisoned by partisan suspicions, even the most well-intentioned deviation from instructions appeared to the president an act of betrayal.

But if the relentless bickering between Polk and his subordinates was unseemly, even puerile at times, it paled in comparison to the irreconcilable differences that existed among Mexico's political elite. The war gave rise to a wave of bitter recriminations, leaving the country more deeply divided than ever before. While many leaders directed their rage at the United States, others placed at least partial blame on Mexico's chronic political instability, which had produced no less than six presidents since the crisis began. The ease with which Scott's small army had invaded the country and seized the capital prompted some to doubt whether Mexico could be called a nation at all. Wrote one disconsolate Mexican politician of his countrymen: "everyone without exception behaved in such a manner that we richly deserve the scorn and derision of all cultivated peoples. We are nothing, absolutely nothing."

CHAPTER

11

Epilogue

Polk had never wavered in his decision to serve only one presidential term. Even so, many prominent Democrats refused to take the president at his word. As the 1848 Democratic convention approached, many urged him to reconsider, insisting that he was the only man who could keep the party together. But the president remained unmoved by these entreaties; after four years in office, Polk looked forward to his retirement. He had recently sold his holdings in Maury County and purchased the Nashville home of his former mentor, Felix Grundy, which was now being readied for his return. "I am heartily rejoiced that my term is so near its close," the weary president confided to his diary, and none who knew him could have doubted his sincerity. Polk's health, never robust, had deteriorated under the burdens of high office. His face creased and careworn, the president looked far older than his 52 years. James Buchanan was struck by the haggard, almost sepulchral countenance of the man once nicknamed "Young Hickory." "[I]n the brief period of four years," the secretary of state noted, Polk "had assumed the appearance of an old man."

The Democrats assembled in Baltimore to choose a candidate in late May. To put an end once and for all to rumors that he might consent to run for a second term, the president drafted a letter that was read to the convention

before the balloting began. Polk refused to endorse any of
the presidential hopefuls, although he had had enough of
James Buchanan's persistent maneuvering for the party's
highest honor and privately favored Michigan senator
Lewis Cass. A strong expansionist, the 65-year-old Cass
won the nomination on the fourth ballot. As had been the
case four years earlier, the party that had once united behind Andrew Jackson was now riven by internal dissension. The split in the New York Democratic party between
the Van Burenites and their enemies had grown so wide
that both groups sent separate delegations to the convention. Unwilling to divide the party still further, the Democratic platform studiously avoided taking a stand on the
issue of slavery in the territories, although Cass's well-
known opposition to the Wilmot Proviso served to dampen
the enthusiasm of free-soil Democrats for the new party
standard-bearer.

As for the Whigs, their nomination of Zachary Taylor
represented a calculated effort to return to the formula
that had won them the presidency with William Henry
Harrison eight years earlier. Many northern Whigs found
Taylor, a Louisiana slaveholder, a repugnant candidate,
but given the electorate's fondness for military heroes they
had to admit that the crusty general offered the party its
best hope to regain the White House. Even more cautious
than the Democrats, the party adjourned without bother-
ing to adopt a platform.

As the 1848 presidential campaign got underway, the
Polk administration continued to push its expansionist
agenda. Strangely oblivious to the sectional rancor that
had been a by-product of its conquest of the West, the
Polk administration now directed its attention toward the
Caribbean basin. For some years the Yucatán peninsula
had been embroiled in an on-again, off-again struggle for
independence. In defiance of Mexico City, the Yucatán

government had remained neutral during the recent conflict with the United States. When a bloody caste war erupted between Maya Indians and *criollo* landowners, the Yucatán government appealed to the United States to extend sovereignty over the region. Polk had hitherto shown little interest in Yucatán affairs; the matter suddenly became one of grave concern, however, when he learned that the Yucatán might ask European powers for assistance if American aid was not forthcoming. Although the region was still a part of Mexico, the president was determined once again to uphold the Monroe Doctrine and take whatever steps necessary to ensure that the peninsula did not "fall into the hands of England." In Congress, expansionist Democrats called for the temporary military occupation of the region, but the Whigs denounced the scheme as a violation of the Treaty of Guadalupe Hidalgo. When an armistice between the Yucatán government and Maya insurgents brought peace to the area, at least for the present, the administration promptly shelved the plan.

The flurry of interest in the Yucatán also revived a project that had tantalized the apostles of Manifest Destiny for many years: the acquisition of Cuba. Once again, the fear of Great Britain dominated expansionist thinking. Rumors that Spain might surrender the island as payment of its debt to London bond holders raised anew the specter of a larger British presence in the western hemisphere. Such a prospect was particularly troubling to southern slave owners, who continued to fret that Britain was engaged in a plot to undermine their labor system. Having failed to abolish slavery in Texas, southern leaders argued, Britain now hoped to accomplish the same objective in Cuba, where the plantation system was firmly established. Fearful that emancipation in Cuba would incite a wave of rebellions throughout the South, slave owners urged Washington to acquire the island. According to southern thinking, such a policy would not only foil the designs of British abolitionists, it would also increase the political power of the Deep South and offer new economic vistas for its planter class, thus ensuring the future security of the American slave empire.

In May, while the Senate was debating the Yucatán question, Illinois senator Stephen Douglas and *Democratic Review* editor John L. O'Sullivan met with the president to discuss the possibility of an American offer to purchase Cuba from Spain. Characteristically tight-lipped, Polk favored the idea but refrained from expressing his views with his visitors. On May 30 he broached the subject for the first time to the cabinet and found it receptive to such a scheme. Accordingly, the administration authorized its minister in Madrid to inform the Spanish government that the United States was willing to pay $100 million for Cuba, warning Spain that under no circumstances would the United States allow Cuba to fall into the hands of a European power. The Spanish foreign minister scornfully dismissed the idea, noting that before it ceded Cuba to any nation, Spain "would prefer seeing it sunk in the Ocean." On that note Polk's expansionist program came to an end.

On July 4, 1848, the president received word that the treaty of Guadalupe Hidalgo had been ratified by the Mexican Congress and promptly issued a proclamation declaring an end to the war. Polk did not yet know it, but the United States had won far more than 500,000 square miles of land and important commercial outlets on the Pacific coast. Within weeks, American vessels returning from California brought the first rumors that gold had been discovered in the Sacramento Valley. Initially, the reports seemed too fantastic to be believed, but in early December a small quantity of gold from the California mines was received in Washington by Secretary Marcy and shown to the president. In the gold rush mania that followed, American production of the precious mineral increased eightfold. A decade later, prospectors found extensive silver deposits in Nevada, and American silver production experienced a thirtyfold increase. Much of this newfound mineral wealth would ultimately be invested in railroads and manufacturing, accelerating the nation's transition from an agricultural economy to an industrial giant. Once again, Americans had reason to believe that theirs was a nation favored by Providence.

But there was a hidden price for these spoils of war. The end of the conflict with Mexico had not silenced the war's opponents; nor had it brought about a return of national harmony. Ironically, while the U.S.–Mexican War established the United States as a hemispheric empire, it also had a corrosive effect on the bonds that held the Union together. Abolitionist Charles Sumner believed that "The Mexican War has hastened by 20 or 30 years the question of slavery." As the war drew to a close, Ralph Waldo Emerson noted with telling prophesy: "The United States will conquer Mexico, but it will be as the man swallows the arsenic, which brings him down in turn. Mexico will poison us."

The nation's attempt to digest the territories seized from Mexico was already producing serious convulsions. Ominously, myths and misconceptions impaired the outlook of political leaders on both sides. Now that the war was over, northerners found new evidence to confirm their suspicions that the crisis had been engineered by the "slave power" to expand its domain. Though John C. Calhoun had opposed the war, he was no less determined to fight northern efforts to prohibit slavery in any of the lands the United States had recently acquired. While both sections agreed that for reasons of climate and geography slavery would never thrive in the West, southerners opposed on principle any effort to impose legal restrictions such as the

Wilmot Proviso, fearful that this would set a precedent for future assaults against their cherished institution.

The incendiary nature of the problem became apparent when Congress attempted to create a territorial government for Oregon. In December 1847, the House of Representatives, where non-slaveholding states held a commanding majority, proposed a bill excluding slavery in Oregon based on the Northwest Ordinance (which in 1787 had prohibited the entry of slaves into the Midwest). The move ran into frenzied opposition from southern legislators. Answering the free-soilers' Wilmot Proviso with his own Resolutions on the Slave Question, John C. Calhoun set forth a southern position that was equally uncompromising. Congress did not have the constitutional right to prohibit the extension of slavery anywhere in the territories, he argued, since the land was the common property of all the states. To bar slave owners from migrating there would deprive southerners of their rights as American citizens.

When it became clear that no solution to the problem would be forthcoming from Congress, Polk sought to break the deadlock. After some indecision the administration adopted the view that slavery should be excluded in Oregon on the basis of the Missouri Compromise, since the territory lay north of the 36°30' line. Southern hardliners were loath to accept this proposal, however, holding fast to the view that Congress did not have the right to exclude slavery under any circumstances. To further complicate matters, Democratic presidential candidate Lewis Cass offered his own compromise solution, the so-called popular sovereignty doctrine, which proposed that the residents of a territory should be allowed to decide for themselves whether the area should be slave or free.

Congress continued to wrestle with the issue of an Oregon territorial bill throughout the summer of 1848. At the close of the session in August, an exhausted Senate finally yielded to a House move to exclude slavery in Oregon on the basis of the Northwest Ordinance, over the objections of Calhoun and other southern legislators. The South Carolina senator pleaded with the president to veto the bill, but Polk refused. Though frustrated and angry by the refusal of free-soilers in the House to accept the principle of the Missouri Compromise, the president was anxious to establish a territorial government in Oregon as soon as possible. Sticking to his position that the Missouri Compromise represented the best solution to the territorial dilemma, Polk signed the measure. The president insisted, however, on sending a message to Congress to make it plain that his approval did not constitute an endorsement of the Northwest Ordinance, but rather was based only on the fact that Oregon lay well above the 36°30' line.

While these deliberations were reaching a climax in Washington, Polk received distressing political news. A motley collection of northern Democrats, Conscience Whigs, and delegates of the Liberty party met in Buffalo, New York, to form the Free Soil party. Adopting the Wilmot Proviso as the main plank in its platform, the new party nominated Martin Van Buren for president. Van Buren had been one of the master builders of the Jacksonian Democratic coalition, and his decision to break rank was a stunning development for party stalwarts like Polk. The president was now beginning to grasp the ominous implications of the growing sectional crisis. The emergence of purely regional parties, he observed with alarm, "must prove dangerous to the harmony if not the existence of the Union itself. . . ." At the same time, however, the self-righteous president was inclined to ascribe only the basest motives to those whose conduct he did not understand. "Mr. Van Buren's course is selfish, unpatriotic, and wholly unexcusable."

Such defections within the Democratic ranks doomed the party in November. Taylor won the election handily, with the Whigs carrying the all-important state of New York, as well as Pennsylvania, where the unpopular Walker tariff cost the Democrats dearly. Significantly, the Free Soil party garnered 10 percent of the vote, almost five times as many votes as the Liberty party had won four years earlier, a sign of the northern electorate's growing dissatisfaction with Democratic and Whig waffling on the slavery issue. The two-party system remained intact, but the election results offered a troubling portent of the sectional crisis to come.

In the waning months of his administration, the lame duck president continued to spend long hours at his desk, attending to the voluminous paperwork and innumerable petty tasks that had consumed so much of his time during the past four years. Polk performed these tedious duties, such as the signing of hundreds of certificates of merit awarded to enlisted men for distinguished service in the Mexican War, without complaint. But he was driven to distraction by the parade of office-seekers who, even in the twilight of his administration, continued to troop through the White House in the hopes of obtaining presidential favors. News of job vacancies spread with astonishing speed. One hour after learning that the U.S. army paymaster had died, Polk received an application to fill the post of the deceased; several more applications would arrive at the White House by the end of the day.

Of greatest concern to Polk during his final days in office was the need to establish federal authority over California and New Mexico. With gold prospectors pouring into California by the thousands, Polk called on Congress to act promptly. Hoping to prevent a repeat of the controversy over the Oregon territorial bill and deny extremists on both sides the opportunity to debate the issue of slavery in the territories, the administration favored the immediate admission of California as a state. Once again, however, the question became mired in the growing sectional controversy. Free-soilers in the House of Representatives had the votes to press for a territorial bill that would exclude slavery in the area, a move that the Senate and Polk found unacceptable. Polk was deeply troubled by the unyielding attitude of both sides. When one representative suggested to the president that the territorial issue might be left to the incoming administration, Polk's curt reply underscored the seriousness of the situation: "I told him we had a country to save as well as a party to obey, and that it was the solemn duty of the present Congress to settle the question."

In the closing days of the second session, a committee composed of members of both houses worked feverishly to break the deadlock, to no avail. In a last-ditch effort to extend federal jurisdiction over California and New Mexico, the Senate attached a rider to a general appropriations bill providing for temporary government in the two territories. The House accepted the proposal, with the proviso that Mexico's laws would remain in force until superseded by Congress. This action threw southern politicians into an uproar, Mexico having abolished slavery in 1829. Polk, who had gone over to the Capitol to sign any bills enacted in the final hours before Congress was scheduled to adjourn, conferred hurriedly with his cabinet for advice on an appropriate response should the bill pass both houses. Though four members urged him to sign such a bill into law, Polk viewed the House measure as the Wilmot Proviso in a new guise, and resolved to veto the legislation. The Thirtieth Congress ended on an anticlimactic note, however, when the controversial amendment was removed from the appropriations bill at the last minute, allowing Polk to sign the measure. Unable to reach an agreement on the question of slavery in the territories, Congress adjourned, leaving the whole issue in doubt and confusion.

March 3 was Polk's last day at the White House. Conscientious to the end, the president worked at his desk until sundown, signing commissions for military, naval, and civil appointments. The first family then checked in to a nearby hotel, where the president would continue to perform his official duties until Taylor's inauguration. "I disposed of all the business on my table down to the minutest detail," Polk wrote with considerable satisfaction in his diary that evening, "and at the close of the day left a clean table for my successor."

In fact, Polk was leaving the new Whig administration with a problem so intractable—the status of slavery in the Mexican Cession—that it would precipitate the most serious political crisis the nation had yet faced. For almost two decades, both major parties had managed to maintain national coalitions by deftly sidestepping the slavery question. By 1849, however, the controversy had assumed center stage, elbowing aside the economic issues over which the two parties had traditionally clashed, such as the bank, internal improvements, and the tariff. Ironically, it was these troubling sectional tensions that Democratic expansionists had hoped to neutralize, by using Manifest Destiny to forge a new political consensus. But the acquisition of lands that had once been the domain of Mexico had flushed the slavery issue out into the open, driving statesmen of both parties into opposing regional camps. Although Mexico had relinquished California and New Mexico in the Treaty of Guadalupe Hidalgo, for 16 months the territories remained in a curious state of limbo, subject only to the authority of a temporary military government. In 1850 an intricate but fragile compromise solution would be pieced together, by which California was admitted as a free state and New Mexico as a territory, forestalling the specter of disunion for another decade.

Polk handed the reins of government over to Zachary Taylor with as much graciousness as he could manage given their stormy relationship during the recent war. What satisfaction Polk felt on being relieved of the burdens of public life was no doubt tempered by the fact that the electorate had repudiated the Democratic party at the polls—an indirect rebuff of his own administration—in favor of a man he regarded as a second-rate general and an amateur politician. On inauguration day, March 5, Polk accompanied the president-elect in an open carriage to the Capitol. During the course of the short ride, Taylor made the casual remark that California and Oregon were too distant from Washington to be part of the United States and should be allowed to establish separate governments. Too stunned to reply, Polk said nothing, but he could not help noting peevishly in his diary that he found Taylor to be "a well meaning old man. He is, however, uneducated, exceedingly ignorant of public affairs, and, I should judge, of very ordinary capacity."

The Polks left Washington that evening, boarding a steamboat with their two nieces and a small entourage. Bowing to the many requests of southern supporters, Polk had agreed to make a month-long tour of the South before returning to Nashville. A number of Democratic congressmen also accompanied the president, departing for home at various stops along the way. Huge and enthusiastic crowds greeted the president as he traveled by boat and train through Virginia, North Carolina, and South Carolina. Despite his carefully cultivated image of republican humility, Polk had always been gratified by the respect and honor paid him by his countrymen. Now free of his presidential responsibilities, Polk thoroughly enjoyed himself, characterizing the trip as a "triumphal march."

But what began as a pleasant excursion soon became a painful, almost nightmarish ordeal. As the Polks made their way across the Deep South, a grueling schedule of galas, parades, and speeches, combined with unseasonably warm weather, began to take their toll on the ex-president's health. By the time he reached New Orleans, Polk was suffering from an acute intestinal disorder and chronic diarrhea. Adding to the ex-president's anxiety, a cholera epidemic had recently broken out in the port city. Carried on the passenger ships arriving from Europe, the epidemic would wreak havoc on communities large and small throughout the United States in the spring and summer months of 1849. Polk wished to sail upriver without delay, but the mayor and other dignitaries prevailed on him not to change his itinerary, pointing out that elaborate preparations had already been made on his behalf. Not wishing to offend his hosts, Polk relented, and for the next two days he struggled vainly to keep up appearances, suffering in silence through several receptions and banquets. The very sight of the rich, exotic French cuisine prepared in his honor made him nauseous, however, and at one reception Polk quietly asked an obliging waiter to bring him some cornbread and broiled ham.

As Polk journeyed by steamboat up the Mississippi, his condition grew steadily worse. He refused to leave the boat, summoning several physicians at stops along the way. Their assurances that he did not have cholera offered the ailing Polk little comfort, while their prescribed medications provided little relief. At last unable to go any farther, Polk disembarked and took rooms at a Smithland, Kentucky, inn. Four days later, weak and exhausted but feeling well enough to undertake the final two-day leg of his journey, the former president boarded a boat for Nashville, where he was greeted by cheering crowds on April 2.

In the weeks that followed, Polk's spirits, if not his health, returned. Shortly after his arrival, Polk journeyed to Columbia and Murfreesboro to visit friends and relatives.

On his return to Nashville, Polk kept himself busy supervising the teams of workmen he had engaged to renovate his new home, now renamed Polk Place. He tended to his library, arranged his presidential papers, and frequently took walks into town, where he enjoyed renewing old acquaintanceships. But with the advent of summer, the cholera epidemic that had first appeared along the Gulf spread rapidly through the South, from New Orleans up the Mississippi River and its tributaries. By late May, the disease had resulted in several deaths in Nashville. His health already broken, Polk succumbed quickly.

On his deathbed, the former president made one last request. Having never been baptized, Polk summoned John B. McFerrin, the Methodist minister whose camp revivals had so moved Polk in earlier years. Jane Knox Polk hurried from her home at Columbia with her own Presbyterian pastor in tow when she learned of her son's illness, but Polk insisted on being received into the Methodist church. McFerrin performed the rite of baptism shortly before the end. Polk died on June 15, 1849.

The expansionist impulse did not die with Polk; he was, after all, an agent of Manifest Destiny, not its creator. In spite of the fact that slavery and expansion had proven to be a highly combustible mixture, some Democrats called for new territorial acquisitions in the decade that followed. Four years after Polk stepped down from the presidential chair, New Hampshire-born Franklin Pierce would attempt to woo southern support by seeking to annex Hawaii and Cuba. Predictably, these abortive efforts elicited an angry response from northerners, who once again accused the Democratic party of surrendering to southern interests.

Thereafter, Manifest Destiny faded from the national agenda, but it would continue to play a vital part in the increasingly bitter sectional conflict. Viewing northern opposition to the expansion of slavery as a direct assault on the institution itself, southerners would grow ever more determined to enlarge the boundaries of the slave empire. Abandoning the cautious expansionism of John C. Calhoun—who had died in 1850—slaveholding extremists called for a territorial crusade to save the South from ruin. Unable to enlist the aid of the national government, they backed filibustering expeditions against Cuba and Nicaragua, while the Knights of the Golden Circle, a secret society, revived the expansionist dream of acquiring Mexico. In the years after Polk's death, Manifest Destiny would become sectionalized; the South's expansionist appetite would become an addiction. In the end, the drive to extend the national domain had not strengthened the Union, as Polk had hoped; it had aggravated the tensions that would sunder it.

However one evaluates his presidency, there can be little doubt that James K. Polk was a strong chief executive. He maintained a firm grip on the reins of government during his four years in office, never deviating from the path down which he wanted to lead the nation. Polk infused a moribund executive branch with a vigor and a sense of direction that the nation had not seen since Andrew Jackson and would not see again until Abraham Lincoln. In domestic policy, the president forced Congress to accept an economic program based on the principles of strict construction and limited government. As commander-in-chief, Polk supervised every facet of the nation's first foreign war. Most important of all, he redrew the map of the United States; with the annexation of Texas, the settlement of the Oregon boundary and the Mexican Cession, Polk added 1.2 million square miles to the national domain, an increase of more than 60 percent.

Few could have predicted that such dynamic leadership would have been possible at the outset of his presidential term. Whereas Jackson and Lincoln presided over vital, newly formed political coalitions eager to test their power, Polk inherited a party apparatus rent by internal discord. The lack of discipline within the party ranks was exacerbated by the controversial circumstances surrounding Polk's dark-horse nomination in 1844, prompting some Democratic leaders to question his legitimacy as the party's standard-bearer. To these handicaps should be added Polk's colorless personality, a serious drawback for any politician.

And yet Polk managed to rise above these limitations. An activist president, he possessed an astonishing capacity for hard work, an implacable resolve, and a consummate faith in his political principles. Polk set the agenda for his presidency; the tests and trials he faced as chief executive were not thrust on him but were, to a large degree, the challenges of his own design. Calling for "a plain and frugal government" and the bold pursuit of American territorial claims in his inaugural address, Polk could point to significant accomplishments in both areas four years later. Few presidents have ever had so clear a view of their goals at the outset of their terms; fewer still can claim to have left the office having fulfilled them.

Despite his impressive record, historians remain divided over Polk's accomplishments. Some have taken issue with the methods he employed, noting that Polk's pious self-righteousness often disguised a calculating, devious nature. He was occasionally less than truthful in his relations with Congress, while his squabbles with subordinates at times seemed petty and mean-spirited. His brinkmanship policy during the Oregon crisis brought the United States perilously close to a needless and potentially disastrous conflict with Great Britain. Of all the indictments against him, Polk's policy toward Mexico has invited the sharpest criticism. His bullying of a weaker neighbor, the violation of its territorial sovereignty, and finally his decision to wage a war of conquest on the spurious grounds of national defense rank among the more controversial chapters in the annals of American international relations.

Polk's achievements are all the more difficult to evaluate in light of their long-term consequences. No sooner had the Treaty of Guadalupe Hidalgo been signed than the Union began to slide slowly but inexorably toward the vortex of civil war. With characteristic stubborness, Polk refused to see the connection between expansion and the slavery controversy. Ironically, the goal-oriented managerial style that may well have been his greatest asset was in large part responsible for this myopia. He could focus intently on objects close at hand, but oftentimes lacked the breadth of vision to see obstacles that lay on the distant horizon.

On Polk's behalf, it should be pointed out that the upheaval that gripped the nation in 1861 looms large only in retrospect. To be sure, the annexation of Texas served notice to leaders of both parties that expansion was an issue dangerously freighted with sectional discord. But when Polk took office in 1845, anti-slavery groups seemed to represent a vocal minority, and it was not unreasonable to suppose that a more broadly defined territorial agenda would win over Democrats not yet committed to the Manifest Destiny crusade. Events would prove him wrong, for beneath the rising tide of nationalism lay strong sectional undercurrents that threatened to destroy the Union. Polk was neither the first public figure nor the last who failed to grasp this paradox.

In the final analysis, Polk's triumphs and his failures were uniquely American ones. The expansionist impulse that defined his presidency was more than the by-product of an exaggerated sense of national destiny—it was a new chapter of an old story, in which the American republic struggled to define itself in an era of rapid change. Its roots can be traced to a nostalgic desire to preserve an agrarian world that was rapidly giving way to a commercial one; to a concern that hallowed principles of limited government were being undermined by a trend toward political consolidation; by a deep-seated, almost pathological distrust of anti-democratic forces, foreign and domestic. One of the hallmarks of the Jacksonian era was the pervasive fear among white Americans that the republican system as they knew it might not endure. This uncertainty helped to foster a political climate of crisis and intense partisanship, one that produced determined ideologues who believed the fate of the nation lay in their hands. Polk's conduct toward Mexico and his willingness to ignore ominous portents of sectional strife must be viewed in this context; the defense of his republican vision outweighed all other concerns.

In this era of change and uncertainty, Polk never wavered in his course, nor questioned the wisdom of his convictions. He looked back to a simpler time for the answers to an increasingly complex world, never doubting for a moment that they could be found there. But despite his imperturbable demeanor, Polk exhibited many of the same contradictions that beset the nation at large. Driven by an overwhelming desire to distinguish himself, Polk was nonetheless disturbed by the rampant self-interest of his generation. Though consumed by personal ambition, he subscribed to a set of traditional values that stressed public duty and social obligation. A staunch Jacksonian, he never fully embraced the ethos of individualism that the Jacksonian revolution had helped to create.

Polk embodied, too, his nation's arrogant cultural chauvinism and its dreams of empire. At the same time he seemed to have given little thought to what the consequences might be if those dreams were realized. Not only was Polk heedless of the strains his continentalist agenda would place on the two-party system; he also failed to grasp that a policy of imperialism necessarily entailed a new, greatly expanded role for the United States on the world stage. Polk had staked a claim for the nation as a hemispheric power, and yet like so many Americans he lacked the international perspective to fully comprehend the magnitude of that achievement. Instead he held fast to a pastoral, provincial view of America, a vision of the future that was deeply rooted in an agrarian past. Polk never faced these inner contradictions; the nation's struggle to resolve them, on the other hand, had only just begun.

Study and Discussion Questions

Chapter One: The New Arcadia

1. How did the Polk family manage to acquire wealth and social prominence in North Carolina and Tennessee? Why was the American Revolution an important event for the clan, enabling it to secure its position among the backcountry elite?

2. What major crisis did Polk face during his early teenage years?

3. What impact did the Panic of 1819 have on American political life?

4. What were the influences that shaped Polk's political beliefs during his early adulthood?

5. What were Polk's strengths as a politician? What were his weaknesses?

Chapter Two: Servant of the People

1. Why was the political climate in Washington such a contentious one during Polk's early years as a congressman?

2. What position did Polk take in the nullification crisis?

3. What was the relationship between Polk and his younger siblings?

4. How did Polk supplement his congressional income?

5. To what extent did Polk's strong religious views impinge upon his business interests as a slaveowner?

6. Raised a Presbyterian, Polk nonetheless evinced a strong attraction to Methodism. How did Polk's interest in Methodist doctrines reflect his democratic ideology? How did his Presbyterian upbringing reflect a very different view of human nature?

7. Why did President Jackson oppose renewing the charter of the Bank of the the United States? How was this political controversy finally resolved? What role did Polk play in this crisis?

Chapter Three: The Shrine of Party

1. Although no longer president, Andrew Jackson continued to have a polarizing effect on American politics. How did Polk's loyalty to the former president affect his ambitions to become Speaker of the House?

2. What were the ideological issues that defined the Democrats and Whigs? How did the composition of these two parties differ?

3. How did Polk's allegiance to his party reflect his opinion of society at large? To what extent was there an element of hypocrisy in his insistence that party loyalties must always come before personal ambition?

4. What was the most controversial issue Polk faced as Speaker of the House?

5. Why were many Tennessee Democrats less than enthusiastic about the election in 1836?

6. What were the political motives behind Polk's decision to resign the speakership and run for governor of his home state? To what extent did personal considerations weigh in his decision?

7. Why did Polk's political career appear to be over by 1843?

Chapter Four: "The Most Available Man"

1. Why were many Democrats unhappy with Van Buren as their party's 1844 presidential convention approached? What specific issue caused many Democrats to reject him as the party's standard bearer on the eve of the convention?

2. What role did Robert J. Walker play in defeating the Van Buren nomination?

3. Why was James K. Polk an ideal compromise candidate for the Democrats in 1844?

4. What important promise did Polk make after the convention in an effort to appease competing factions within the Democratic Party?

5. Why was choosing a cabinet so difficult for Polk? What factors influenced his cabinet appointments?

Chapter Five: "I Am the Hardest Working Man in This Country"

1. Why did Polk's first actions as president antagonize some members of his own party?

2. How would you characterize Polk's managerial style as president? In what ways did the new president maintain a tight grip over his administration and his subordinates?

3. Historians have often used the term "imperial presidency" to describe the trappings of power associated with the modern executive branch. How did the daily operations of the White House during Polk's presidency reflect a very different attitude toward presidential authority?

4. What was Polk's attitude toward his social obligations as president? Did he enjoy his years as president?

5. Polk had always been committed to the Jeffersonian idea of limited republican government, believing that no interest group should receive special favors from the nation's lawmakers. How was this political philosophy reflected in his domestic policies?

Chapter Six: The Course of Empire

1. What is meant by the term "Manifest Destiny"?

2. Why did eighteenth-century Americans have misgivings about territorial expansion?

3. What factors fueled Americans' territorial appetites in the early decades of the nineteenth century? Which of these factors, according to the author, was the most important?

4. What racial arguments did expansionists use to justify their territorial agenda?

Chapter Seven: All of Texas and All of Oregon

1. Why were relations between the United States and Mexico so tense after Mexico won its independence? How did the Texas Revolution aggravate these problems?

2. What role did Great Britain play in fueling tensions between the United States and Mexico?

3. Why did Polk instruct Zachary Taylor to station his army below the Rio Grande? Why was this such a controversial move?

4. Why did Polk believe an aggressive policy toward Mexico would be successful?

5. Why did Polk believe California was ripe for American expansion? Why was he especially interested in acquiring the territory at this time?

6. What did Polk hope his new minister to Mexico, John Slidell, would accomplish? What issue was Slidell not allowed to discuss with Mexican leaders? Why was Polk's optimism regarding the Slidell mission unwarranted?

7. Although Mexico had asked Washington to send an envoy to resolve outstanding grievances between the two countries, the Herrera government refused to accept him when he arrived. Why?

8. The United States and Great Britain both claimed possession of the Oregon boundary territory when Polk took office. Why were expansionists in the Democratic party opposed to any form of compromise on this issue?

9. Why did negotiations with Great Britain over the Oregon boundary come to an abrupt halt shortly after Polk took office? What was Britain's response to this unexpected turn of events?

10. What was so extraordinary about Polk's positions with regard to Oregon and Texas, as articulated in his first annual message?

Chapter Eight: "Hostilities Have Commenced"

1. Why did Polk reverse his earlier instructions to John Slidell regarding the potential purchase of California from Mexico?

2. Why did Polk believe he had grounds for war against Mexico even before he learned of hostilities along the Rio Grande?

3. Although many Whigs believed the war with Mexico was unjustified, they still voted for the war bill. Why?

4. Why was Polk anxious to resolve the Oregon boundary dispute with Great Britain in the spring of 1846?

5. Why did Polk's similarly aggressive policies toward Britain and Mexico produce such different outcomes?

6. Some historians have accused Polk of bullying Mexico into a war. Is this a valid assessment?

Chapter Nine: Mr. Polk's War

1. To what extent did domestic party politics play a role in the U.S. offensive against Mexico?

2. What were Pennsylvania congressman David Wilmot's reasons for seeking to prohibit slavery in the territories acquired from Mexico?

3. Why was Polk unhappy with Taylor's performance as commander of U.S. forces in Mexico, despite his victories on the battlefield?

4. In what region of the country was opposition to the war strongest?

5. Why did Polk decide to invade central Mexico? What were the risks involved in such a strategy?

6. Examine Polk's strengths as commander-in-chief of the nation's first foreign war. What were his weaknesses?

Chapter Ten: Conquering a Peace

1. What was the purpose of the Trist mission to Mexico? Why did Polk believe the U.S. diplomat would be a suitable representative of his administration?

2. Why did Scott's drive toward the Mexican capital stall after the Battle of Cerro Gordo?

3. Why did some expansionists believe the United States should annex all of Mexico?

4. What was the reason for the rupture between Polk and Nicholas Trist?

5. In the end, how much territory did the United States acquire from Mexico?

Chapter Eleven: Epilogue

1. What other territories did Polk consider acquiring as the war with Mexico drew to a close? Why did he believe extending U.S. sovereignty over these territories was necessary?

2. Why did sectional tensions develop over the question of slavery in Oregon, despite the widely held belief that slavery could never exist there? What was Polk's position on this issue?

3. According to the author, what were Polk's principal accomplishments as president? What challenges did he face that other strong executives during the nineteenth century did not?

4. Why have historians had such difficulty evaluating Polk's presidency in spite of all he managed to accomplish during his four years in office?

5. To what extent did Polk embody the contradictions of the nation at large during the Jacksonian era?

Bibliographical Essay

Students of Polk's career have a rich mine of primary materials to explore. As of this writing, ten volumes of *The Correspondence of James K. Polk*, Weaver, Bergeron, Cutler, et al., eds., have been published, covering Polk's career up to December 1845, his first year in office. Pending the publication of volumes that deal with the remainder of Polk's White House years, his presidential correspondence is available only on microfilm (Papers of James K. Polk, Washington: Library of Congress, 1964, 67 reels). The *House Journals, Congressional Globe,* and the *Register of Debates* are indispensable tools for Polk's 14-year tenure as a Tennessee representative from the Nineteenth to the Twenty-fifth Congress, 1825–1839. Unquestionably the most valuable single source of information on Polk is his presidential diary. Published in four volumes, *The Diary of James K. Polk during his Presidency, 1845 to 1849*, Milo M. Quaife, ed. (Chicago: A. C. McClurg & Co., 1910) offers a detailed day-by-day account of the Polk White House, and goes far to illuminate the personality of a man often described by contemporaries as aloof and impenetrable. For Polk's official addresses and messages to Congress, see James D. Richardson, *A Compilation of the Messages and Papers of the Presidents, 1789–1899*, vol. 4 (Washington, DC: U.S. Congress, 1898).

Several important studies of Jeffersonian agrarian society, politics, and the trans-Appalachian frontier help to place Polk's upbringing in North Carolina and Tennessee in a broader context. See, for example, Lance Banning, *The Jeffersonian Persuasion: Evolution of a Party Ideology* (Ithaca: Cornell University Press, 1978); Drew McCoy, *The Elusive Republic: Political Economy in*

Jeffersonian America (Chapel Hill: University of North Carolina Press, 1980); Malcolm J. Rohrbough, *The Trans-Appalachian Frontier: People, Societies and Institutions, 1775–1850* (New York: Oxford University Press, 1978); Thomas Abernethy, *From Frontier to Plantation in Tennessee* (Chapel Hill: University of North Carolina Press, 1932).

For a readable history of the Polk clan from its arrival in America to the 20th century, see William Polk, *Polk's Folly: An American Family History* (New York: Doubleday, 2000). The best study of Polk's early years remains the first volume of Charles Grier Sellers's biography *James K. Polk, Jacksonian, 1795–1843* (Princeton: Princeton University Press, 1957). Other studies that provide useful information on the future president's early years include Tennessee Historical Commission, *Tennessee, Old and New,* vol. 1 (Kingsport: Kingsport Press, 1946); Stanley J. Folmsbee, Robert E. Coslew, and Enoch C. Mitchell, *History of Tennessee,* vol. 1 (New York: Lewis Historical Publishing Co., 1960); Phillip M. Hamer, ed., *Tennessee. A History, 1673–1932,* vol. 1 (New York: American Historical Society, 1933); Robert W. Ickard, "Surgical Operation on James K. Polk by Ephraim McDowell, or the Search for Polk's Gallstone," *Tennessee Historical Quarterly,* 43(1984), 121–131; "The Boyhood of President Polk," Albert V. Goodpasture, *Tennessee Historical Magazine,* 7 (April 1921–January 1922), 38–50; Anson and Fanny Nelson, *Memorials of Sarah Childress Polk, Wife of the Eleventh President of the United States* (New York: Anson D. Randolph, 1892); Daniel A. Tompkins, *History of Mecklenberg County and the City of Charlotte from 1740 to 1903,* 2 vols. (Charlotte, NC: Observer Printing House, 1903).

Accounts of Washington, D.C. in the early decades of the nineteenth century used in this study are drawn from Charles Dickens, *American Notes; and Pictures from Italy* (rev. ed., New York: Oxford University Press, 1987); Constance McLaughlin Green, *Washington, Village and Capital, 1800–1878,* vol. 1 (Princeton, NJ: Princeton University Press, 1962); Fanny Kemble, *Journal of a Young Actress* (New York: Columbia University Press, 1990); and John William Reps, *Washington on View: The Nation's Capital Since 1790* (Chapel Hill: University of North Carolina Press, 1991). Finally, an unfavorable assessment of Polk's role as slavemaster is examined in William Dusinberre's *Slave Master President: The Double Career of James Polk* (New York: Oxford University Press, 2003).

Excellent overviews covering Jacksonian society and politics are Glyndon G. Van Deusen, *The Jacksonian Era, 1828–1848* (New York: Harper & Brothers, 1959); Charles Grier Sellers, *The Market Revolution: Jacksonian America, 1815–1846* (New York: Oxford University Press, 1991); Harry L. Watson, *Liberty and Power: The Politics of Jacksonian America* (New York: Hill and Wang, 1990). Important general works on the Jacksonian republican identity include Marvin Meyers, *The Jacksonian Persuasion; Politics and Belief* (Stanford, CA: Stanford University Press, 1960); Edward Pessen, *Jacksonian America: Society, Personality, and Politics,* rev. ed. (1978); and Arthur M. Schlesinger, Jr., *The Age of Jackson* (Boston: Little, Brown, 1945). More specialized political studies of the period include M. J. Heale, *The Presidential Quest: Candidates and Images in American Political Culture, 1787–1852* (London: Groveman Group, 1982); Michael F. Holt, *Political Parties and American Political Development, from the Age of Jackson to the Age of Lincoln* (Baton Rouge: Louisiana State University Press, 1992); Richard P. McCormick, *The Second American Party System: Party Formation in the Jacksonian Era* (Chapel Hill: University of North Carolina Press, 1966); and Joel H. Silbey, *The Shrine of Party: Congressional Voting Behavior, 1841–1852* (Pittsburgh: University of Pittsburgh Press, 1964).

For information on Polk's career as a Tennessee congressman and governor, see Paul H. Bergeron, *Antebellum Politics in Tennessee* (Louisville: University Press of Kentucky, 1982); "The Diaries of S. H. Laughlin, of Tennessee, 1840, 1843," *Tennessee Historical Magazine,* 2 (March–December 1916); Oliver P. Temple, *Notable Men of Tennessee from 1833 to 1875: Their Times and Their Contemporaries* (New York: Cosmopolitan Press, 1912). For additional information on the feud between Polk and John Bell, see Joseph Howard Parks, *John Bell of Tennessee* (Baton Rouge: Louisiana State University Press, 1950); and Norman L. Parks, *The Career of John Bell as Congressman from Tennessee, 1827–1941* (Nashville: Joint University Libraries, 1942). Polk's religious views are discussed in John Berry McFerrin, *A History of Methodism in Tennessee* (Nashville: Southern

Methodist Publishing House, 1869); and O. P. Fitzgerald, *John B. McFerrin, A Biography* (Nashville: Publishing House of the Methodist Episcopal Church, South, 1889). For more information on life on Polk's plantations in Tennessee and Mississippi see John Spencer Bassett, *The Southern Plantation Overseer, as Revealed in His Letters* (New York: Negro Universities Press, 1968).

The best study of the controversial 1844 Democratic nominating convention and the campaign that followed is James C. N. Paul's *Rift in the Democracy* (Philadelphia: University of Pennsylvania Press, 1957). For more on Polk's contemporaries in the Democratic party see Frederick Moore Binder, *James Buchanan and the American Empire* (Selinsgrove, PA: Susquehanna University Press, 1994); John M. Belohlavek, *George Mifflin Dallas: Jacksonian Patrician* (University Park: Pennsylvania State University Press, 1977); Donald B. Cole, *Martin Van Buren and the American Political System* (Princeton, NJ: Princeton University Press, 1984); John Arthur Garraty, *Silas Wright* (New York: Columbia University Press, 1949); Philip Klein, *President James Buchanan: A Biography* (University Park: Pennsylvania State University, 1962); James P. Shenton, *Robert John Walker; A Politician from Jackson to Lincoln* (New York: Columbia University Press, 1961); Ivor D. Spencer, *The Victor and the Spoils: A Life of William L. Marcy* (Providence: Brown University Press); Charles M. Wiltse, *John C. Calhoun,* 3 vols. (Indianapolis, 1929); and Frank B. Woodford, *Lewis Cass, the Last Jeffersonian* (New Brunswick, NJ: Rutgers University Press, 1950).

Much of the information on Polk's daily routine is culled from *The Diary of James K. Polk* and, to a lesser extent, from *Memorials of Sarah Childress Polk,* both of which are cited above. Also helpful is William Seale, *The President's House, A History,* vol. 1 (Washington, DC: White House Historical Association, 1986). For more information on Sarah Childress Polk, see John Reed Baumgarner, *Sarah Childress Polk: A Biography of the Remarkable First Lady* (Jefferson, TN: McFarland & Company, 1997).

A number of secondary works deal specifically with Polk's years as the 11th president. The most recent is Paul H. Bergeron, *The Presidency of James K. Polk.* The second volume of Charles Grier Sellers' biography *James K. Polk, Continentalist,* is an excellent study of Polk's first two years in the White House, but does not include his role as commander-in-chief during the Mexican-American War years. Other studies include Lucien B. Chase, *History of the Polk Administration* (New York: George P. Putnam, 1850); John S. Jenkins, *James Knox Polk, and a History of His Administration* (Auburn: John E. Beardley, 1850). Polk's problems with the spoils system are examined in Norman Graebner, "James K. Polk: A Study in Federal Patronage," *Mississippi Valley Historical Review* 38 (1951–1952). Also useful for their analysis of Polk's managerial style are Charles A. McCoy, *Polk and the Presidency* (Austin: University of Texas Press, 1960); and Leonard D. White, *The Jacksonians: A Study in Administrative History, 1829–1861* (New York: Macmillan, 1954).

The dynamics of American territorial growth have been examined by scholars from a variety of perspectives. Studies of early U.S. expansionism include: Donald Jackson, *Thomas Jefferson and the Stony Mountains: Exploring the West from Monticello* (Urbana: University of Illinois Press, 1981); and William Earl Weeks, *John Quincy Adams and American Global Empire* (Lexington: University of Kentucky Press, 1992). Albert K. Weinberg's path-breaking study, *Manifest Destiny: A Study of Nationalist Expansion in American History* (Baltimore: Johns Hopkins University Press, 1935) remains one of the best analyses of this phenomenon. Other contributions to the historiography of American expansion are: Norman A. Graebner, *Empire on the Pacific: A Study in American Continental Expansion* (New York: Ronald Press Company, 1955); Thomas R. Hietala, *Manifest Design: Anxious Aggrandizement in Late Jacksonian America* (Ithaca: Cornell University Press, 1985); Frederick Merk, *Manifest Destiny and Mission in American History* (New York: Alfred A. Knopf, 1963); and *The Monroe Doctrine and American Expansionism, 1843–1849* (New York: Alfred A. Knopf, 1966); and Anders Stephanson, *Manifest Destiny: American Expansionism and the Empire of Right* (New York: Hill and Wang, 1995). See also John Higham, *From Boundlessness to Consolidation: The Transformation of American Culture, 1848–1860* (Ann Arbor, MI: William L. Clements Library, 1969). Students seeking an overview of the nation's 11th president may also wish to consult two recent biographies: Thomas M. Leonard's *James K. Polk, A Clear and Unquestionable Destiny*

(SR Books, 2000), and John Seigenthaler's *James K. Polk* (New York: Times Books, 2003).

The following newspapers were consulted for this book and provide a selective sampling of the jingoistic tenor of the expansionist press: the *Daily Madisonian* (Washington, DC); New Orleans *Daily Picayune;* New York *Herald;* New York *Morning News; Telegraph and Texas Register* (Houston); and Washington *Union.* The *U.S. Magazine and Democratic Review,* though more restrained than the "penny press," is also an important source for expansionist propaganda of the period. Anglo-American attitudes toward Mexicans in the early decades of the nineteenth century are the focus of David J. Weber, "Scarce More Than Apes," *New Spain's Far Northern Frontier: Essays on Spain in the American West, 1540–1821,* David J. Weber, ed. (Dallas: Southern Methodist University Press, 1988); James Ernest Crisp, "Anglo-Texan Attitudes Toward the Mexican, 1821–1845" (Ph.D. diss., Yale University, 1976); Arnoldo De León, *They Called Them Greasers: Anglo Attitudes Toward Mexicans in Texas, 1821–1900* (University of Texas Press, 1983); and Reginald Horsman, *Race and Manifest Destiny: The Origins of American Racial Anglo-Saxonism* (Cambridge: Harvard University Press, 1981).

The most thorough and well-balanced study of the diplomacy during the Tyler and Polk administrations is David Pletcher's *The Diplomacy of Annexation: Texas, Oregon, and the Mexican War* (Columbia: University of Missouri Press, 1973). Still useful is Justin H. Smith's exhaustive *The Annexation of Texas* (New York: Baker and Taylor Company, 1911). See also Ephraim D. Adams, *British Interests and Activities in Texas, 1838–1846* (Gloucester: Peter Smith, 1963); William W. Freehling, *The Road to Disunion: Secessionists at Bay, 1776–1854* (New York: Oxford University Press, 1990); Frederick Merk, *Fruits of Propaganda in the Tyler Administration* (Cambridge: Harvard University Press, 1971); and *Slavery and the Annexation of Texas* (New York: Knopf, 1972). For more on the role of anti-British sentiment as a factor in U.S. expansionist policies, see Sam W. Haynes, "Anglophobia and the Annexation of Texas: The Quest for National Security," in Sam W. Haynes and Christopher Morris, eds., *Manifest Destiny and Empire: American Antebellum*

Expansionism (College Station: Texas A&M University Press, 1997); and Sam W. Haynes, "'But What Will England Say?' Great Britain, the United States, and the War with Mexico," in Richard Francaviglia and Douglas W. Richmond, eds., *Dueling Eagles: Reinterpreting the U.S.–Mexican War, 1846–1848* (Fort Worth: Texas Christian University Press, 2000).

The Polk administration's expansionist policies are discussed in a number of important collections of official and private correspondence including: John Spencer Bassett, *Correspondence of Andrew Jackson*, vol. 6 (Washington, DC: Carnegie Institute of Washington, 1926–35); George Hammond, ed., *The Larkin Papers: Personal, Business, and Official Correspondence of Thomas Oliver Larkin, Merchant and United States Consul in California*, vol. 10 (Berkeley: University of California Press, 1964); William R. Manning, *Diplomatic Correspondence of the United States, Inter-American Affairs, 1831–1860*, vol. 8 (Washington, DC: Carnegie Endowment for International Peace, 1937); John Bassett Moore, ed., *The Works of James Buchanan*, vol. 6 (New York: Antiquarian Press, 1960); "Letters of James K. Polk to Andrew J. Donelson, 1843–1848," *Tennessee Historical Magazine* 3(March–December, 1917); Amelia W. Williams and Eugene C. Barker, eds., *The Writings of Sam Houston, 1813–1863* (Austin: University of Texas Press, 1938–1943); Clyde N. Wilson, ed., *The Papers of John C. Calhoun*, vols. 17–22 (Columbia: University of South Carolina Press, 1990).

Other useful diaries and memoirs that help to shed some light on American public opinion during the 1840s and which are quoted in this work include Thomas Hart Benton, *Thirty Years' View* . . . (New York: D. Appleton, 1854); Thomas Jefferson Green, *Journal of the Texian Expedition against Mier*, Sam W. Haynes, ed. (Austin: Thomas Taylor Publishing, 1992); Allan Nevins, ed., *The Diary of Philip Hone, 1828–1851* (New York: Dodd, Mead, 1936); Ralph H. Orth and Alfred R. Ferguson, eds., *The Journals and Miscellaneous Notebooks of Ralph Waldo Emerson, 1843–1847*, vol. 9 (Cambridge: Harvard University Press, 1971); Benjamin B. French, *Witness to the Young Republic: A Yankee's Journal* (Hanover: University Press of New England, 1989); Beverly Wilson Palmer, ed., *The Selected Letters of Charles Sumner*, vol. 1 (Boston: Northeastern University Press, 1940);

Theodore Parker, *Sermons on War by Theodore Parker . . .* (New York: Garland, 1973); Charles Wilkes, *The Autobiography of Rear Admiral Charles Wilkes, U.S. Navy, 1798–1877,* William James Morgan et al., eds. (Washington, DC: Naval History Division, Department of the Navy, 1978).

A good reference work on the U.S.–Mexican War is *The United States and Mexico at War: Nineteenth Century Expansionism and Conflict* (New York: Macmillan, 1998). Useful overviews of the causes of war between the United States and Mexico can be found in Thomas Benjamin, "Recent Historiography of the Origins of the Mexican War," *New Mexico Historical Review,* 54 (1979), 169–181; and Ward McAfee, "A Reconsideration of the Origins of the Mexican-American War," *Southern California Quarterly,* 62 (1980), 49–65. The most exhaustive history of the U.S.–Mexican War remains Justin Smith's *The War with Mexico,* 2 vols. (New York: Macmillan, 1919), although its value is diminished by its unabashedly pro-American viewpoint. Two more recent military histories are K. Jack Bauer, *The Mexican War, 1846–1848* (New York: Macmillan, 1974), and John D. Eisenhower, *So Far From God* (Random House: 1989). Anna Kasten Nelson, *Secret Agents: President Polk and the Search for Peace with Mexico* (New York: Garland, 1988) examines the Polk administration's diplomatic initiatives to end the war. The life of the common soldier is examined in James McCaffrey's *Army of Manifest Destiny: The American Soldier in the Mexican War* (New York: New York University Press, 1992); and Richard Bruce Winders, *Mr. Polk's Army: The American Military Experience in the Mexican War* (College Station: Texas A&M University Press, 1997).

A large number of eyewitness accounts of the U.S.–Mexican War have been published. For biographies of Winfield Scott, see Timothy D. Johnson, *Winfield Scott: The Quest for Military Glory* (Lawrence: University Press of Kansas, 1998); and John S. D. Eisenhower, *Agent of Destiny: The Life and Times of General Winfield Scott* (New York: Free Press, 1997). For more on the diplomatic initiatives to resolve the war with Mexico, see Anna Kasten Nelson, *Secret Agents: President Polk and the Search for Peace with Mexico* (New York: Garland Publishing, 1988); and Wallace Ohrt, *Defiant Peacemaker: Nicholas Trist in the Mexican War* (College Station: Texas A&M University Press, 1998).

The travails and frustrations of the American soldier in the Mexican War are the focus of several books; see Paul Foos, *A Short, Offhand, Killing Affair: Soldiers and Social Conflict During the Mexican–American War* (Charlotte: University of North Carolina Press, 2002); Richard Bruce Winders, *Mr. Polk's Army: The American Military Experience in the Mexican War* (College Station: Texas A&M University Press, 1996); and James McCaffrey, *Army of Manifest Destiny: The American Soldier in the Mexican War* (New York; New York University Press, 1992). Among those consulted for this book are Samuel Chamberlain, *My Confession, The Recollections of a Rogue* (Lincoln: University of Nebraska Press, 1987); Ethan Allen Hitchcock, *Fifty Years in Camp and Field: Diary of Major-General Ethan Allen Hitchcock, U.S.A.* (G. P. Putnam's Sons, 1909); George B. McClellan, *The Mexican War Diary of George B. McClellan* (Princeton, NJ: Princeton University Press, 1917); George Gordon Meade, *The Life and Letters of George Gordon Meade* (New York: Charles Scribner's Sons, 1913); George Winston Smith and Charles Judah, *Chronicles of the Gringos: The U.S. Army and the Mexican War, 1846–1848, Accounts of Eyewitnesses and Combatants* (Albuquerque: University of New Mexico Press, 1968); and Irving W. Levinson, *Wars Within a War: Mexican Guerillas, Domestic Elites, and the United States of America, 1846–1848* (Fort Worth: Texas Christian University, 2005).

Robert W. Johannsen's *To the Halls of the Montezumas: The Mexican War in the American Imagination* (New York: Oxford University Press, 1985) offers an insightful study of the war as seen by the American public. John H. Schroeder examines criticism of the administration's Mexico policy in *Mr. Polk's War: American Opposition and Dissent, 1846–1848* (Madison: University of Wisconsin Press, 1973). Also helpful in understanding New England opposition is Kinley J. Brauer, *Cotton versus Conscience, Massachusetts Whig Politics and Southwestern Expansion* (Lexington: University of Kentucky Press, 1967); while Ernest McPherson Lander, Jr., focuses on southern criticism of Polk's expansionist goals in *Reluctant Imperialists: Calhoun, the South Carolinians, and the Mexican War* (Baton Rouge: Louisiana State University Press, 1980). For more on Polk's tour of the Northeast in 1847, see Wayne Cutler, *North for*

Union: John Appleton's Journal of a Tour to New England Made by President Polk in June and July, 1847 (Nashville: Vanderbilt University Press, 1986). The All Mexico movement is the focus of John D. P. Fuller, *The Movement for the Acquisition of All Mexico, 1846–1848* (Baltimore: Johns Hopkins University Press, 1936).

Mexican perspectives of the war can be found in Dennis Berge, "The Mexican Response to United States' Expansionism, 1841–48" (Ph.D. diss., University of California at Berkeley, 1965); Gene Martin Brack, *Mexico Views Manifest Destiny, 1821–1846: An Essay on the Origins of the Mexican War* (Albuquerque: University of New Mexico Press, 1975); Homer C. Chaney, Jr., "The Mexican–United States War, As Seen by Mexican Intellectuals, 1846–1956" (Ph.D. diss., Stanford University, 1959); Thomas Ewing Cotner, *The Military and Political Career of José Joaquín de Herrera, 1792–1854* (Austin: University of Texas Press, 1949); Cecil Robinson, *The View from Chapultepec: Mexican Writers on the Mexican–American War* (Tucson: University of Arizona Press, 1989); Pedro Santoni, *Mexicans at Arms: Puro Federalists and the Politics of War* (Fort Worth: Texas Christian University Press, 1996).

The impact of the treaty ending the U.S.–Mexican War is examined by Donald C. Cutter, "The Legacy of the Treaty of Guadalupe-Hidalgo," *New Mexico Historical Review,* 1978 53(4): 305–315; and Richard Griswold del Castillo, *The Treaty of Guadalupe-Hidalgo: A Legacy of Conflict* (Norman: University of Oklahoma Press, 1990). The sectional tensions provoked by the Polk administration's policies of expansion have been studied by a number of scholars, but among the most incisive analyses are those offered by Michael F. Holt, *The Political Crisis of the 1850s* (New York: W. W. Norton, 1978); and David Potter, *The Impending Crisis* (New York: Harper & Row, 1976).

Index